50 INSTRUCTIONAL STRATEGIES
To Build Student Engagement & Participation

STETSON & ASSOCIATES, INC.

281.440.4220
14343-G Torrey Chase Blvd.
Houston, Texas
www.stetsonassociates.com

50 INSTRUCTIONAL STRATEGIES
To Build Student Engagement & Participation

TABLE OF CONTENTS

Forward	vii.
How to Use This Book	ix.
Strategy Rubric	x.
Student-Directed Learning Environments	xii.

#1	2x10	1
#2	Anticipation Guide	2
#3	Bingo Lingo	3
#4	Classroom Expectations	4
#5	Class Mosaic	5
#6	Concept/Definition Map	6
#7	Conversation Circles	7
#8	Cornell Notes	8,9
#9	Cubing	10
#10	Curriculum Compacting	11
#11	Differentiated Lecture	12
#12	Extension Menu	13,14
#13	Find Someone Who…	15
#14	Flexible Grouping	16
#15	Four Corners	17
#16	Gallery Walk	18
#17	Give One – Take One	19
#18	Graffiti Wall	20
#19	Graphic Organizers	21
#20	Highlighted Text	22
#21	Inside-Outside Circles	23
#22	Interactive Notebooks	24
#23	Jigsaw	25
#24	Little Foldable Booklet	26
#25	Mindstreaming	27
#26	Mix & Mingle	28
#27	Motivational Mentor	29
#28	One-Sentence Summary	30
#29	Pop Quiz Swap	31
#30	Portfolio Assessment	32
#31	Pre-Teaching Vocabulary	33
#32	Previewing	34
#33	Prompt Sequence	35
#34	Q&A Consensus	36
#35	RAFT	37
#36	Response Cards	38
#37	Round Robin	39
#38	Rubrics	40
#39	Selective Highlighting	41
#40	Socratic Questioning	42
#41	Sticky Note Questions	43
#42	Task Analysis	44
#43	Text Quest	45
#44	Think Fast!	46
#45	Think Pair Share	47
#46	Tiered Learning	48
#47	Visual Schedules	49
#48	Windowpane	50
#49	Word Alert	51
#50	WordSplash	52

50 INSTRUCTIONAL STRATEGIES
To Build Student Engagement & Participation

FORWARD

Have you ever attended a training session where you found your mind wandering?

Have you ever watched students in your class start to check out and stop participating after a few minutes?

Effective teachers know that student engagement starts to decrease when whole group lecture lasts for long spans of time. In fact, research tells us that children can only pay attention for 10-12 minutes before their minds begins to wander. The challenge for a teacher is to use that information to help them design lessons that promote active participation and lead to deeper learning.

A simple Internet search will no doubt reveal hundreds of instructional strategies teachers can use in their lessons, but it is not as simple as just learning a new strategy. Effective teachers select instructional strategies that work in the lesson and with THEIR students. The purpose of this book is to introduce and describe 50 instructional strategies that promote active learning. On each strategy sheet you will find a simple, easy to understand description, practical examples and tips for implementing the strategy in your classroom. As you design your classroom instruction, consider the points in the lesson where you have an opportunity to build in active learning. Some of the strategies may help you to differentiate the process of how you are going to teach the concept. Others may give you ideas for allowing students to show their learning in different ways.

Have some fun and try something new! Think about the learning needs of each of YOUR students and select a strategy that enhances your lesson. Spend some time reflecting on the experience. What went well? Is there anything that you would do differently next time? Did it encourage active participation by 100% of your students? What will you try next?

Be the teacher you always wanted to have!

50 INSTRUCTIONAL STRATEGIES
To Build Student Engagement & Participation

HOW TO USE THE 50 STRATEGIES BOOK

Teachers have several decisions to make when designing lessons. The curriculum tells us what to teach, but how it will be taught depends on the learning needs of the students in the classroom. The questions facing the teacher are:

- What do my students already know about this topic? (pre-assessment)
- What instructional strategies will I use to teach the information? (process)
- How will I measure learning? (product)
- Do any students have an IEP that modifies the curriculum? (content)
- Is the environment in my classroom conducive to learning? (learning environment)

The following rubric gives ideas about how to use the 50 strategies included in this book. Each strategy is included in the table as well as an idea for the most common use of the strategy. If you are looking for new ideas for pre-assessment, look through the list and focus on the strategies that are most frequently used for pre-assessment.

As you get more and more comfortable with expanding your repertoire of differentiated strategies you will find that most, if not all, of the strategies can be used at any point in the lesson sequence. This rubric is intended to help you get started and to make your planning more efficient and effective.

STRATEGY RUBRIC

	STRATEGY	PRE-ASSESSMENT	CONTENT	PROCESS	PRODUCT	LEARNING ENVIRONMENT
1	2x10					X
2	Anticipation Guide	X		X	X	
3	Bingo Lingo	X			X	
4	Classroom Expectations					X
5	Class Mosaic	X		X	X	X
6	Concept Definition/Mapping	X	X	X	X	
7	Conversation Circles	X	X	X	X	
8	Cornell Notes			X		
9	Cubing	X	X	X	X	
10	Curriculum Compacting	X	X			
11	Differentiated Lecture			X		X
12	Extension Menu		X	X	X	
13	Find Someone Who…	X		X		
14	Flexible Grouping			X		X
15	Four Corners	X		X	X	
16	Gallery Walk	X		X	X	
17	Give One – Take One	X		X	X	
18	Graffiti Wall	X		X	X	
19	Graphic Organizers	X	X	X	X	
20	Highlighted Text		X	X		
21	Inside-Outside Circles	X		X	X	
22	Interactive Notebooks			X	X	
23	Jigsaw	X		X		
24	Little Foldable Booklet	X		X	X	
25	Mindstreaming	X		X		

© 2016, Stetson & Associates, Inc.

	STRATEGY	PRE-ASSESSMENT	CONTENT	PROCESS	PRODUCT	LEARNING ENVIRONMENT
26	Mix & Mingle	X	X			
27	Motivational Mentor		X	X	X	
28	One-Sentence Summary	X			X	
29	Pop Quiz Swap			X		
30	Portfolio Assessment		X		X	
31	Pre-Teaching Vocabulary	X	X		X	
32	Previewing	X				
33	Prompt Sequence		X	X	X	X
34	Q&A Consensus	X	X	X		
35	RAFT		X	X	X	
36	Response Cards	X		X	X	
37	Round Robin	X		X	X	
38	Rubrics	X	X		X	
39	Selective Highlighting		X	X		
40	Socratic Questioning	X		X	X	
41	Sticky Note Questions	X		X		
42	Task Analysis	X	X		X	
43	Text Quest	X		X		
44	Think Fast!	X		X		X
45	Think Pair Share	X		X		X
46	Tiered Learning		X	X	X	
47	Visual Schedules			X		X
48	Windowpane	X		X	X	
49	Word Alert	X		X		
50	Wordsplash	X		X	X	

© 2016, Stetson & Associates, Inc.

50 INSTRUCTIONAL STRATEGIES
To Build Student Engagement & Participation

STUDENT-DIRECTED LEARNING ENVIRONMENTS

Have you ever taught a lesson that you thought was going to be great, but the students just didn't seem to be paying attention?

An important factor in today's classroom is the engagement level of our students and their response to the instruction that is being delivered in the classroom. Consider the value of student directed learning environments. Is there some way that you can give students more input into their own learning needs?

Student-directed learning results in classrooms where academic learning time is increased.

More Academic Learning Time = More Learning

Students who are taught and provided support to participate in student-directed learning environments learn self-determination skills through applying new concepts in ways that impact their lives directly.

In a student-directed learning environment students set their learning goals, monitor their own progress and manage the quality of the learning environment. Self-recording and self-monitoring has shown improvement in motivation and performance for students of all ages and grade levels.

© 2016, Stetson & Associates, Inc.

When creating a student-directed learning environment, the teacher guides students through a series of questions to help them evaluate their own need, make a plan, and evaluate their progress:

SET A LEARNING GOAL: (BEFORE INSTRUCTION)
1. What do I want to learn?
2. What do I already know about it now?
3. What must change to learn what I do not know?
4. What can I do to produce that change?

CONSTRUCT A LEARNING PLAN: (DURING INSTRUCTION)
1. What can I do now to change what I do not know?
2. What will prevent me from taking action now to produce change?
3. What can I do to remove these obstacles?
4. When will I take action and remove the obstacles?

ADJUST BEHAVIOR: (REFLECTION AFTER INSTRUCTION)
1. What actions have I taken?
2. What obstacles have been removed?
3. What has changed about what I do not know?
4. Do I know what I wanted to know?

Resources:

Chamberlin, M. (May 2001), Implementing self-determination activities. Remedial and Special Education.

Flexer, R., Simmons, T., Luft, P., Baer, R. (2005, 2nd Ed.). Transition planning for secondary students with disabilities. Upper Saddle River, NJ: Pearson Merrill Prentice Hall.

Hughes, C. (June 2000). A national survey of teachers' promotion of self-determination and student-directed learning. Journal of Special Education.

2X10 (TWO BY TEN)
Strategy 1

Two by Ten is a strategy for building authentic relationships and assessing student needs. Applied strategically, the teacher formally, though subtlety, meets with the student and "conducts" a two-minute personal conversation about anything the student is interested in on a daily basis for 10 consecutive days. The teacher listens to the student and later may make note of information that will help reach the learner.

IMPLEMENTATION

1. Choose students to target for this approach. Any student can be chosen, but students who are not responding to instruction, not engaging in learning, struggling academically and are having behavior difficulties are often selected.

2. Create a simple note-taking tool to record when the behavior occurs and a few notes about the conversation.

3. Meet with the student for 2 minutes. Begin with a conversation starter and then LISTEN to the student responses.

4. Extend responses by restating what the student said, or comment about what the student said showing interest, not judgment.

5. Make note of the conversation identifying significant information to guide the next meeting.

HOT TIPS

• The focus is to build a relationship with the student.

• Focus on the student's interests.

• Avoid emotionally charged topics.

• Maintain a positive and supportive approach when interacting with the student.

• Listen, listen, listen!

• Watch for signs of discomfort.

• Use information from Student Interest Surveys to generate conversation starters.

• Use observation and "I noticed that..." statements to generate responses.

EXAMPLE

Date	Conversation Topics	Reflection

© 2016, Stetson & Associates, Inc.

ANTICIPATION GUIDE
Strategy 2

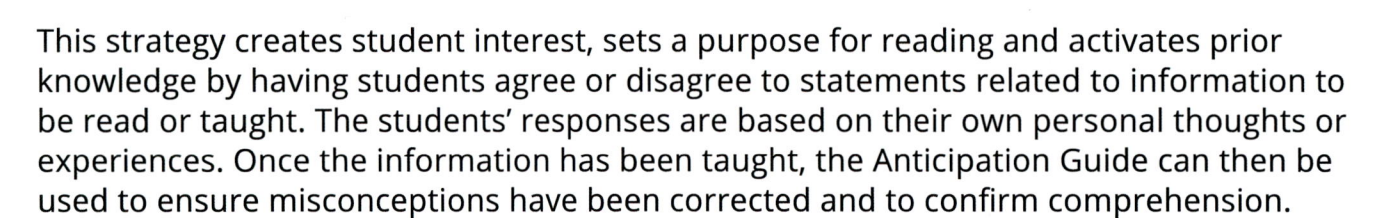

This strategy creates student interest, sets a purpose for reading and activates prior knowledge by having students agree or disagree to statements related to information to be read or taught. The students' responses are based on their own personal thoughts or experiences. Once the information has been taught, the Anticipation Guide can then be used to ensure misconceptions have been corrected and to confirm comprehension.

HOT TIPS

- This strategy can be utilized for non-print media.

- Can be used in most content areas.

- Have students place a sticky note in the text where they find information or evidence to support their responses.

- Create Anticipation Guides from different perspectives (e.g. different characters in a literary selection).

- Have students create the Anticipation Guides.

IMPLEMENTATION

1. Identify the concepts and ideas to be taught. Determine students' experiences and whether the new knowledge to be taught will challenge or support the students' beliefs.
2. Create an "Anticipation" with 4-6 statements which will challenge and support the students' beliefs and experiences. Include a statement that expresses a misconception students may have.
3. Present the Anticipation Guide before reading or direct teach. Emphasize that students are to agree or disagree with the statements.
4. Have students discuss their answers and the justification for their opinions in pairs or small group (about five minutes at the most).
5. Teach information or have students read a selection. Direct them to focus on information that will support or refute the statements in the Anticipation Guide.
6. Have students return to the Anticipation Guide to determine if they still agree with their original choices, locating the text information to support or refute the statement.

Optional: whole class discussion

EXAMPLE

Name: _____ Date: _____

Directions: Read each statement. Mark whether you agree or disagree with the statement in the "Before Reading" column.

Before Reading			In Your Own Words		
Agree	Disagree	Statement	Support	No Support	Page
		1.			
		2.			
		3.			

Directions after Reading: Re-read each statement. If you found information to support your response, put a check in the "support" column and in your own words, write a summary of the information that supported your response. If you found information to disprove your response, check "No Support" and in your own words summarize the correct information.

© 2016, Stetson & Associates, Inc.

BINGO LINGO
Strategy 3

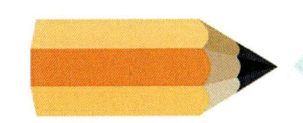

Bingo Lingo is a fun, engaging vocabulary activity that teaches and scaffolds definitions. Students think they are playing a game, while in reality they are reviewing key vocabulary terms.

IMPLEMENTATION

1. Identify critical vocabulary terms students need to understand related to the topic or concept being taught. Be sure to have the dictionary definition as well as a more student-friendly definition to help scaffold. The goal is to ensure that all students understand the meaning of the term.

2. Have students fold a piece of paper in half four times. When the paper is opened there will be 16 boxes. See the graphic below.

3. Have students write down the key words at random in the boxes from the list provided.

4. To play the game, the teacher provides the dictionary definition and then scaffolds as necessary to ensure student understanding. Multiple scaffolds may be necessary depending on students' vocabulary or language knowledge.

5. Students mark the words on their sheets as the game progresses. Rather than having beans, markers or bits of paper, have students color code the grid for each game.

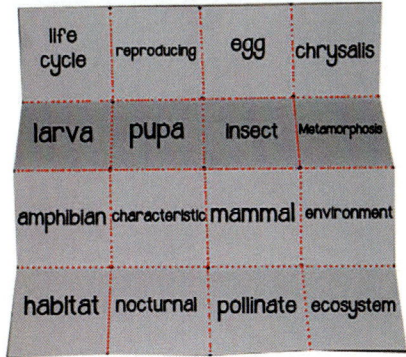

HOT TIPS

• Create a list of 20 key words from which your students will choose 16 terms.

• Scaffold the definitions to make them comprehendable for students.

• Use online tools such as Visual Online Dictionaries like www.snappywords.com and visual.merriam-webster.com.

• Use online tools like http://www.wordhippo.com to find example sentences, synonyms, antonyms, rhyming words, pronunciations and much more.

• Use www.wordsift.org or www.wordle.net to identify key words about the concept being taught.

• Prizes are not necessary. Students just love playing the game.

EXAMPLE

life cycle	reproducing	egg	chrysalis
larva	pupa	insect	Metamorphosis
amphibian	characteristic	mammal	environment
habitat	nocturnal	pollinate	ecosystem

© 2016, Stetson & Associates, Inc.

CLASSROOM EXPECTATIONS
Strategy 4

Classroom rules and procedures create and help to sustain a learning environment in which students feel safe, know what to expect and can take risks. When students actively participate in the creation of these rules and procedures, they have ownership of their classroom.

HOT TIPS

- Don't assume students understand the expectations.

- Have students "act out" or model the expected behavior.

- Allow discussion of the finer points of the expectations to ensure understanding.

- Make your class expectations a class contract signed by all students and teacher.

- Post consequences separately from expectations.

- List procedures and teach them before content is taught. Practice!

IMPLEMENTATION

1. Divide students into groups. Assign roles: Facilitator, Timekeeper and Scribe. Facilitators will direct discussion to key points, Timekeepers will keep groups moving toward completion within a set time, and Scribes will record the group's input.
2. Ask groups to discuss and record their expectations for behavior in the class. What are the expectations for student and teacher behavior? Ask them to think about the atmosphere or feeling they want in their classroom.
3. Reconvene the class as a whole and scribe the group's responses.
4. Once expectations are recorded, create a T-Chart to explicitly teach the expectations.
5. When expectations are clear for the whole class, have students sign the sheet on which the expectations are written.
6. Post the expectations. As new students enter the class throughout the year review the expectations. It is most effective if students are the "teachers" for this review.
7. In a separate session, address consequences and post them.

EXAMPLE

1. Separate procedures from expectations. Determine which procedures you will pre-determine for your classroom and those in which students should have input.

2. Consider each step in the process. Be sure you have materials required for the procedures to work smoothly.

3. Remember, everything should have a place. Teach students where it is.

Class Rules
RESPECT OTHERS

Listen & Follow Directions

WORK QUIETLY

Have a Positive Attitude

always do your best

© 2016, Stetson & Associates, Inc.

CLASS MOSAIC
Strategy 5

Class Mosaic is a class project that addresses cultural awareness and is a celebration of diversity. This strategy helps students to concretely see they are individuals who are also "part of a whole." It also helps to develop cohesiveness and teamwork in the classroom.

Source: Paterson, Kathy, Differentiated Learning: Language and literacy projects that address diverse backgrounds and cultures, Pembroke Publishers Limited, 2005.

IMPLEMENTATION

1. Cut a black paper circle approximately 5 feet in diameter. You may need to piece together paper.
2. Cut a second circle the same size as the first. Divide it into parts by folding in half, then quarters, then eights. Open the second circle and draw a small circle in the center and another circle about halfway from the center point.
3. Cut up the divided portions to make one "tile" per student. If you have too many tiles, offer them to students who want to make more than one. (The tiles do not have to be uniform, just have one per student.)
4. Mark the back of each tile with an X. Student does not color this side.
5. Decorate the small center circle yourself to use as a model, or simply label it with the class name.
6. Introduce the concept of symbols (something that represents or stands for symbols of other cultures are examined, or with young children, omit the component).
7. Invite students to decorate individual tiles in any way that represents them. For example, they might show favorite colors, activities and foods.
8. Collect tiles and have student help glue them to the black background.

HOT TIPS

• Encourage use of symbols specific to students' cultures and words from their home language.

• Alternative tile decorating can include collages of magazine pictures, photographs, and fingerprints with finger paint.

• This activity can be extended by having students include a poem or meaningful quotation on their tiles.

• Use this activity to begin a discussion about "fitting in" and being a part of a group.

• Extend this activity to an examination of parts and whole, fractions and geometry.

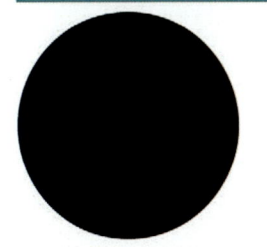

EXAMPLE

1. Cut background circle

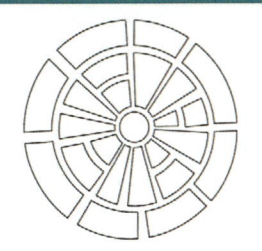

2. Cut mosaic pieces

3. Glue decorated pieces

© 2016, Stetson & Associates, Inc.

CONCEPT/DEFINITION MAP
Strategy 6

Concept/Definition Mapping is an approach that allows students to integrate their knowledge into the definition and understanding of a word or concept. By focusing the learner's attention to the critical components of the concept or word, the student is empowered to integrate it into their own vocabulary. This map can be used: to pre-assess content knowledge, to activate prior knowledge, as a note-taking guide during direct teach and as a post-assessment.

HOT TIPS

• Modify to meet students' needs by adding boxes or partially completing them.

• The picture/symbol box can be an illustration, antonym, synonym, or an example of where the concept is found in life.

• Either words or pictures may be used to demonstrate information or knowledge.

• Color coding the concept/definition mapping components enhances the internalization of the information.

• Modify maps for parts of speech, biographies, definition concepts, and note-taking guides to accompany textbooks.

© 2016, Stetson & Associates, Inc.

IMPLEMENTATION

1. Familiarize students with concept/definition mapping by explaining the components and parts while utilizing a blank template.
2. Model utilization of the concept/definition map by presenting a familiar concept and "thinking aloud" while completing the parts. For example, ice cream is defined as a food or dessert. Its attributes or characteristics are sweet, cold, and creamy. Examples of ice cream are vanilla, chocolate and strawberry. An ice cream cone would be an appropriate illustration.
3. Complete a second concept/definition map eliciting students' input. Use another familiar concept as guided practice.
4. Demonstrate how to write and verbalize a definition utilizing the information on the map.
5. Present new vocabulary words or a concept. During direct teach, complete a concept/definition map or have students complete the form using information from readings. You can assign different words or concepts to students within a cooperative group so they can teach each other.

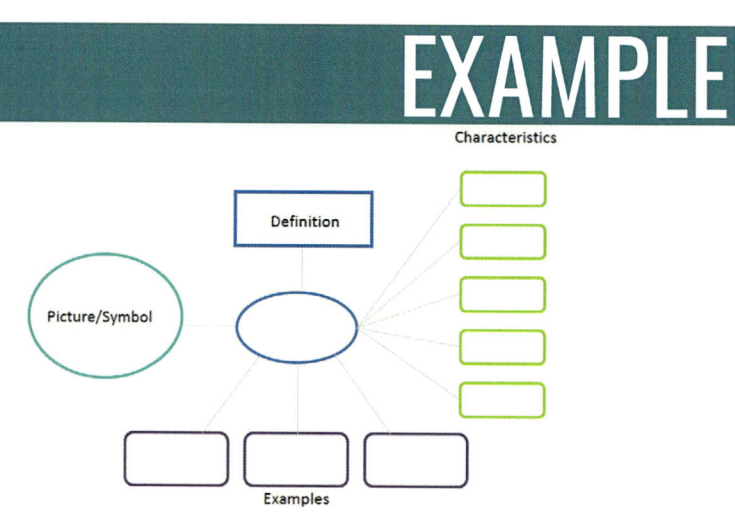

EXAMPLE

CONVERSATION CIRCLES
Strategy 7

This instructional strategy creates groups of three students to discuss their knowledge on a specific topic. This is a simple way to determine their prior knowledge before starting a new unit and requires no special materials, equipment or advance preparation. Students have an opportunity to interact with their peers and learn from each other. Every student is able to participate at their present performance level and make valuable contributions to the group. This structured discussion format also increases social and communication interactions.

IMPLEMENTATION

1. Give each student a piece of paper with three circles on it.
2. Introduce the topic to be discussed and have each student write down what they know about the topic in one of the circles.
3. Place the students into groups of three: Student A, Student B, and Student C.
4. On your cue, Student A shares what they wrote down with their group while the other two students take notes in one of the blank circles on their page.
5. At your signal, Student B starts sharing while the other two students write down the information. At the next signal Student C continues the process.
6. At the end of the third "conversation" all three students in the group have written down the prior knowledge of each of the members in their group.

HOT TIPS

• Have the students write down their thoughts before you place them into groups.
• If you have a student who may not have as much information to share you can construct their group so that this student shares first.
• Have a plan for how you want to place the students into groups before beginning the strategy.
• Once the groups have finished, consider calling on several groups to share with the larger group.
• Check for engagement by having Student A share one idea that they got from Student B.
• Instead of printing paper with three circles, have students fold a piece of paper into three sections and label them A, B, and C.

EXAMPLE

MATH – Students write down everything they remember about fractions.
ELA – Students write down the parts of speech that they remember.
SCIENCE – Students write down as many of the elements that they can remember.
SOCIAL STUDIES – Students write down factors that lead to the Civil War.

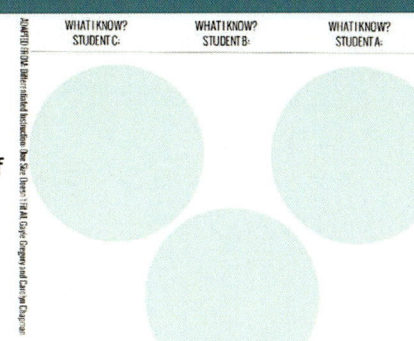

© 2016, Stetson & Associates, Inc.

CORNELL NOTES
Elementary Strategy 8

The Cornell Note-taking method and two column notes are best utilized when information is given in a sequential, orderly fashion. It can be utilized with well-structured main ideas and details, problem-solution and cause-effect relationships. The left column is for the main ideas, questions, key concepts or cues while the right hand column is the note-taking column with the details, definitions, facts, relationships, and/or causes. A summary of the notes is written at the bottom of each page.

HOT TIPS

- Use to focus student's attention during a lecture, direct teach, or reading.
- Use as a study tool or test review.
- Use to record reactions or reflections while reading.
- The notes can be completed with words and/or pictures.
- Use www.mynoteit.com to create a template and allow students to input information via computer. Proficient note-taking students can email the notes to struggling students.

Before: The teacher creates the left hand column of the note-taking guide. It is used to activate prior knowledge or as a pre-assessment.
During: During the direct teach or lecture of a lesson, the student completes the note-taking guide.
After: Use as review, closure or summarization of key concepts presented during the class.

IMPLEMENTATION

1. The teacher makes a digital version of a reading selection and demonstrates how to identify key points.
2. Preview the assignment by reading the introduction and paying close attention to bold print, headings and visuals.
3. Develop a purpose to read.
4. Model how to convert the reading to notes.
5. Demonstrate how to use notes to review information and self-test by using questions and key vocabulary in left column.
6. The same process is followed during a lecture with regard to modeling the note-taking process for students, identifying what is important to include in the notes, demonstrating what to write, how to identify the main ideas or questions and how to study from the notes.

STUDENTS WHO BENEFIT:
- Are confused about what to include and exclude
- Copy all information verbatim
- Experience difficulty maintaining attention, following ideas, or interpreting information presented orally

EXAMPLE

Key Points	Notes
Summary	

Main Idea	Details
What is the circulatory system? How is it different from the digestive system? List 2 functions of this system.	
Summary	

© 2016. Stetson & Associates, Inc.

CORNELL NOTES
Secondary Strategy 8

The Cornell note-taking method and two column notes are best utilized when information is given in a sequential, orderly fashion. It can be utilized with well-structured main ideas and details, problem-solution and cause-effect relationships. The left column is for the main ideas, questions, key concepts or cues while the right hand column is the note-taking column with the details, definitions, facts, relationships, and/or causes. A summary of the notes is written at the bottom of each page.

IMPLEMENTATION

1. The teacher makes a digital version of a reading selection and demonstrates how to identify key points.
2. Preview the assignment by reading the introduction and paying close attention to bold print, headings and visuals.
3. Develop a purpose to read.
4. Model how to convert the reading to notes.
5. Demonstrate how to use notes to review information and self-test by using questions and key vocabulary in left column.
6. The same process is followed during a lecture with regard to modeling the note-taking process for students, identifying what is important to include in the notes, demonstrating what to write, how to identify the main ideas or questions and how to study from the notes.

STUDENTS WHO BENEFIT:
- Are confused about what to include and exclude
- Copy all information verbatim
- Experience difficulty maintaining attention, following ideas, or interpreting information presented orally

EXAMPLE

Key Points	Notes
Summary	

Main Idea	Details
What is the endocrine system? How is it different from other body systems? List each endocrine gland.	
Summary	

HOT TIPS

- Use to focus student's attention during a lecture, direct teach, or reading.
- Use as a study tool or test review.
- Use to record reactions or reflections while reading.
- Notes can be completed with words and/or pictures.
- Use www.mynoteit.com to create a template and allow students to input information via computer. Proficient note-taking students can email the notes to struggling students.

Before: The teacher creates the left hand column of the note-taking guide. It is used to activate prior knowledge or as a pre-assessment.
During: During the direct teach or lecture of a lesson, the student completes the note-taking guide.
After: Use as review, closure or summarization of key concepts presented during the class.

CUBING
Strategy 9

Cubing is an instructional strategy that asks students to consider a concept from a variety of different perspectives. The cubes are six-sided figures that have a different activity on each side of the cube. A student rolls the cube and does the activity that comes up.

HOW TO DIFFERENTIATE CUBING:
- Not all students receive the same cube.
- You can differentiate cubes according to readiness, learning profile or interest.

HOT TIPS

- Cubing gives students who like to move around a chance to feel like they are "playing" while learning.
- Cubing encourages students to look at a concept from a series of different perspectives.
- Cubing allows the teacher to differentiate for readiness in a different way. Since all students are working with cubes, students are not aware that their neighbors might be doing something a little different.
- Use the Cube Creator Tool on www.readwritethink.org

CONCERN:
Cubes can turn into glorified worksheets-but not if all activities are purposeful and focused on getting students to understand a concept in a multitude of ways.

IMPLEMENTATION

1. Students can work alone, in pairs or in small groups with the appropriate cube.
2. In pairs or small groups, each student takes a turn rolling the cube and doing the activity that comes up. Students have the choice to roll again once if they do not like the activity that came up.
3. Students each roll the cube 2-4 times, depending on the magnitude of the assignment(s).

CUBE SIDE SUGGESTIONS:
DESCRIBE IT * COMPARE IT * ASSOCIATE IT * ANALYZE IT * APPLY IT * CONNECT IT * ILLUSTRATE IT * CHANGE IT * SOLVE IT * QUESTION IT * REARRANGE IT * SATIRIZE IT * EVALUATE IT * RELATE IT TO SOMETHING ELSE * CONTRAST IT * INVESTIGATE IT * WHAT IS THE SIGNIFICANCE OF IT? * PUT IT IN HISTORICAL PERSPECTIVE * WHAT ARE THE CAUSE/EFFECTS OF IT? * CARTOON IT * TELL THE PARTS OF IT * ARGUE FOR/AGAINST IT

Adapted from: http://curry.virginia.edu/uploads/resourceLibrary/nagc_cubing__think_dots.pdf

EXAMPLE

SIDE ONE: LOCATE IT	SIDE TWO: DEFINE IT	SIDE THREE: SOLVE IT
In two minutes, make a list of all the places in which we find fractions in every day life. Have your partner time you.	What is a fraction? How would you explain what a fraction is to a first grader?	Complete fraction problems 1-10 on page 64. Have your partner check your work.
SIDE FOUR: ANALYZE IT	**SIDE FIVE: THINK ABOUT IT**	**SIDE SIX: ILLUSTRATE IT**
What are the parts of a fraction? Define each part and describe their relationships to one another.	When dividing fractions, why do we have to "invert and multiply?" Show your thinking on paper.	Create a children's picture book about fractions. Use "Give me Half" as an example.

© 2016, Stetson & Associates, Inc.

CURRICULUM COMPACTING
Strategy 10

Curriculum Compacting is a strategy that identifies student-learning objectives, pre-assesses for prior mastery, and eliminates unnecessary teaching or redundant practice when the student has previously demonstrated mastery of the learning.

IMPLEMENTATION

1. Identify the relevant learning strategies.

2. Develop the assessment of these objectives prior to the beginning instruction.

3. Determine which students should be pre-assessed.

4. Pre-assess. Include sub-areas of specific content, including mastery and non-mastery levels.

5. Eliminate any practice or instruction in which students have achieved the learning objective.

6. Offer acceleration and/or enrichment options for identified students.

HOT TIPS

• Adapts learning to individual levels.

• Provides time on needed instruction rather than previously acquired learning.

• Allows differentiated content from foundation to gifted levels.

• Requires teachers to achieve "focused planning."

• Provides opportunities for students with foundational skills to accelerate learning.

PRE-ASSESSMENT TOOLS

GALLERY WALK
KWL CHART
FOUR CORNERS
CONVERSATIONS CIRCLES
PRE-ASSESSMENT CHECKLISTS
KNOWLEDGE BOARD
SELF-ASSESSMENT
POP QUIZ
GRAPHIC ORGANIZER
RESPONSE CARDS
JOURNALS
CONFERENCING/OBSERVING
BOXING
PAPER PASS
BEHAVIORAL CHECKLIST
READING SURVEY
GRAFFITI FACTS
WHAT I KNOW

© 2016, Stetson & Associates, Inc.

DIFFERENTIATED LECTURE
Strategy II

In a Differentiated Lecture, the instructor provides information to a large or small group of students accompanied by several different strategies. The strategies provide for student reflection, response and involvement through a variety of modalities and methods.

HOT TIPS

- Shorter lecture increments and more active student involvement increases student comprehension and retention.

- This strategy provides students with reflection time to process and transfer information into working memory.

- Differentiated Lecture changes lecture from a passive to an active instructional technique.

- Students typically retain close to 90% of the information presented when allowed to immediately use or teach others as opposed to the 5% retained from traditional lecture.

IMPLEMENTATION

1. Deliver lecture on any subject.

2. Formate the lecture into "mini-lecture" segments of 10-20 minutes using one or more of the activities below:

FEEDBACK LECTURE	Deliver lecture for 10 minutes. Divide students into lecture study groups. Have them complete a pre-determined task based on the information given during the lecture.
OUTLINE COMPLETION	Provide students with a partially completed outline before the commencement of the lecture. Challenge students to follow outline while listening to the lecture and then verbally prompt students to add key information in the blanks provided on their incomplete outline.
GUIDED LECTURE	Provide students with a list of lecture objectives ahead of time. Deliver a 10-minute lecture. Students are not to take notes until the end of the lecture when they write down everything they can remember for 5 minutes. Then students work with partners to fill in any missing information.
RESPONSIVE LECTURE	Students generate questions of their own which form the content of the lecture that lasts from 10-20 minutes.
DEMONSTRATION LECTURE	Give a lecture for approximately 20 minutes that focuses on an interactive demonstration of information to be presented.
PAUSE PROCEDURE LECTURE	Give a lecture for approximately 20 minutes, pausing after the first 10 minutes of information. Give the students 2 minutes to share their notes with a peer to fill in any gaps.
THINK-WRITE-DISCUSS LECTURE	Give students 3 questions during a lecture of 20 minutes – 1 question before, during, and after the lecture. Have students write a response to each question and share the results with a peer. Collect papers at the end of the lecture for personal comments or feedback.

© 2016, Stetson & Associates, Inc.

EXTENSION MENU
Elementary Strategy 12

An extension menu is an array of independent learning activities presented in a "choice" or "menu" format to provide students with options for extending or enriching the essential curriculum.

STUDENTS WHO BENEFIT:
- Have difficulty completing task.
- Need to demonstrate mastery utilizing different learner outcomes.
- Need both choice and challenge.
- Have diverse learning needs.

IMPLEMENTATION

1. Develop learning activities at a variety of appropriate levels on Bloom's Taxonomy.
2. Number boxes so that activities can be assigned based on student ability, interest and learning styles.
3. Provide students with a copy of the rubric prior to the extension menu options.
5. Model the use of an extension menu before expecting students to use one.
6. Share expectations and criteria for evaluating student work.

Adapted from: The Access Center, www.k8accesscenter.org

EXAMPLE

Dinner Menu: Photosynthesis

Appetizer (Everyone Shares)
- Write the chemical equation for photosynthesis.

Entrée (Select One)
- Draw a picture that shows what happens during photosynthesis.
- Write two paragraphs about what happens during photosynthesis.
- Create a rap that explains what happens during photosynthesis.

Side Dishes (Select at Least Two)
- Define respiration, in writing.
- Compare photosynthesis to respiration using a Venn Diagram.
- Write a journal entry from the point of view of a green plant.
- With a partner, create and perform a skit that shows the differences

Dessert (Optional)
- Create a test to assess the teacher's knowledge of photosynthesis.

HOT TIPS

Extension Menus:

- Extend and enrich the essential curriculum

- Address learning styles and student interests

- Encourage self-responsibility and independent thinking skills

• Use wix.com or Google Slides to create a choice board and then share the URL with students.

BEFORE: Teacher decides how to use the extension menu and in which curricular area(s)
DURING: Anchoring activity, Learning center activity, and Independent activity
AFTER: Follow-up activity, Culminating activity, and Study guide

© 2016, Stetson & Associates, Inc.

EXTENSION MENU
Secondary Strategy 12

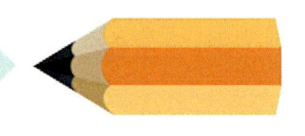

An extension menu is an array of independent learning activities presented in a "choice" or "menu" format to provide students with options for extending or enriching the essential curriculum.

STUDENTS WHO BENEFIT:
- Have difficulty completing task.
- Need to demonstrate mastery utilizing different learner outcomes.
- Need both choice and challenge.
- Have diverse learning needs.

HOT TIPS

Extension Menus:

- Extend and enrich the essential curriculum.

- Address learning styles and student interests.

- Encourage self-responsibility and independent thinking skills.

- Use wix.com or Google Slides to create a choice board and then share the URL with students.

BEFORE: Teacher decides how to use the extension menu and in which curricular area(s)
DURING: Anchoring activity, Learning center activity, and Independent activity
AFTER: Follow-up activity, Culminating activity, and Study guide

IMPLEMENTATION

1. Develop learning activities at a variety of appropriate levels on Bloom's Taxonomy.
2. Number boxes so activities can be assigned based on student ability, interest and learning styles.
3. Provide students with a copy of the rubric prior to the extension menu options.
4. Introduce each different type of learning activity during whole group instruction.
5. Model the use of an extension menu before expecting students to use one.
6. Share expectations and criteria for evaluating student work.

EXAMPLE

DIRECTIONS:
Choose activities in a tic-tac-toe design such as a row or column. As a challenge, keep going and complete extra activities. Star the activities you plan to complete. Color the box when you finish the activity.

Collect	Teach	Draw	Judge
Facts or ideas which are important to you. (Knowledge)	A lesson about your topic to our class. Include as least one visual aid. (Synthesis)	A diagram, map or picture of your topic. (Application)	Two different viewpoints about an issue. Explain your decision. (Evaluation)
Photograph Videotape, or film part of your presentation. (Synthesis)	**Demonstrate** Something to show what you have learned. (Application)	**Graph** Some part of your study to show how many or how few. (Analysis)	**Create** An original poem, dance, picture, song, or story. (Synthesis)
Dramatize Something to show what you have learned. (Synthesis)	**Survey** Others to learn their opinions about some fact, idea, or feature of your study. (Analysis)	**Forecast** How your topic will change in the next 10 years. (Synthesis)	**Build** A model or diorama to illustrate what you have learned. (Application)
Create An original game using the facts you have learned. (Synthesis)	**Memorize** And recite a quote or a short list of facts about your topic. (Knowledge)	**Write** An editorial for the student newspaper or draw an editorial cartoon. (Evaluation)	**Compare** Two things from your study. Look for ways they are alike and different. (Analysis)

© 2016, Stetson & Associates, Inc.

FIND SOMEONE WHO...
Strategy 13

This cooperative learning strategy actively involves all students, helping them learn and master content as well as acquire communication skills. It also encourages peer support and provides review of information by giving students an opportunity to find classmates who may share their knowledge about a given topic.

IMPLEMENTATION

1. Predetermine the question or statement. Consider using technology to create the worksheet or cards.
2. State the purpose of the strategy.
3. Model how the students should engage with one another during this activity.
   a. Students find someone who knows the answer.
   b. Students write the answer in their own words.
   c. Students sign their name next to the response.
   d. Repeat the steps. A student's name can only appear once on a worksheet.
4. Actively monitor to assist and encourage students.
5. Allow approximately 10 minutes.

HOT TIPS

- Use at the beginning of the year to get acquainted, help students review information, master concepts or activate prior information.
- Utilize as a pre-assessment, post-assessment or review of information.
- Pair students if one student needs additional support.
- Students may only sign a classmate's handout once.
- Once a person has obtained an answer, they can then provide the answer to others because they now know the information.
- Have a "fun" question highlighting current events.
- Be sure to teach your students about 3-inch voices, as this can be a loud activity with the entire class talking simultaneously.

EXAMPLE

FIND SOMEONE WHO...	
Has been to the State Fair... tell what it was like. X_____	Owns a pet... share responsibilities. X_____
Has good friends... share qualities. X_____	Has been to a farm... what is it like? X_____

Owns a pet... share responsibilities.
X_____

Has been to a farm... what is it like?
X_____

© 2016, Stetson & Associates, Inc.

FLEXIBLE GROUPING
Strategy 14

Flexible grouping practices provide the teacher with continuous ways to allow students to work at their individual interest levels, readiness levels, and on specific skills identified through classroom diagnosis. Flexible grouping should be short-term and should be based on clear learning objectives and identified student products.

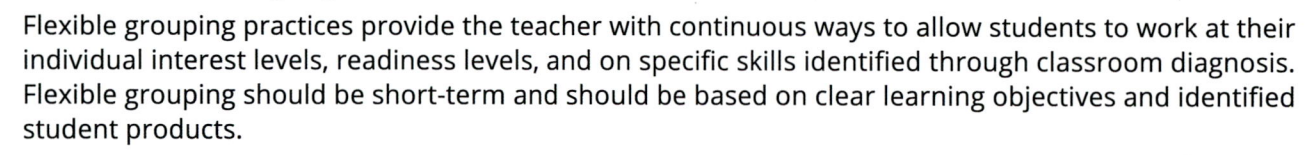

Many traditional classrooms continue to use only whole group instruction – thus leaving many students out of the learning experience. Flexible grouping options expand and enrich instructional delivery and the opportunities for student success.

HOT TIPS

Flexible Grouping:

- Enables the teacher to place students in the best environment for specific learning.
- Allows students to develop positive interpersonal skills.
- Provides small group instruction.
- Allows students to learn within their optimum interest & readiness levels.
- Allows the use of a wide variety of materials at various levels.

- Remember to vary the group membership.

- Name the groups for the work being done.

IMPLEMENTATION

1. Identify the curriculum outcome to be taught.
2. Identify the specific activity to support the learning or outcome.
3. Determine the purpose(s) for grouping students in the activity.
4. Select the method for grouping based upon purpose and anticipated outcomes.
5. Determine the expected student product(s) as a result of the activity.
6. Determine the grading procedure to be used with the groups.
7. Establish group rules & norms and project timelines.
8. Be specific, clear and concise when explaining the projected work to students.
9. Monitor student progress during the activity.

EXAMPLE - GROUPING IDEAS

- Unique situations
- Learning styles
- Reading levels
- Same language
- Small group
- Heterogeneous
- Interest areas
- Physical size
- Random
- Social strengths
- Enrichment
- Math levels
- Gender
- Chronological age
- Culture
- Learning centers
- Peer teaching
- General ability
- Recent assessments
- Prior learning
- Re-teaching groups
- Career choice
- Cooperative groups
- Specific skill level
- Class meetings
- Student choice
- Large group
- Mixed grade
- Skills attainment
- Room size
- Multiple Intelligence
- Pre-teach groups

FOUR CORNERS
strategy 15

Four Corners helps to identify pre-existing knowledge of content, concepts, topics or skills to be studied by students.

IMPLEMENTATION

1. Determine concept, topic, vocabulary, or skill to assess.

2. Draw a rectangle with a center and four sides clearly defined.

3. In the middle of the rectangle place the concept, topic, etc.

4. In each of the side areas place an element of the main concept, or topic to be assessed.

5. Have students respond to the entire sheet, filling in what they know or need to know.

NOTE:
This activity can be used in any grade level by varying the difficulty of the four corners and is appropriate for all content areas.

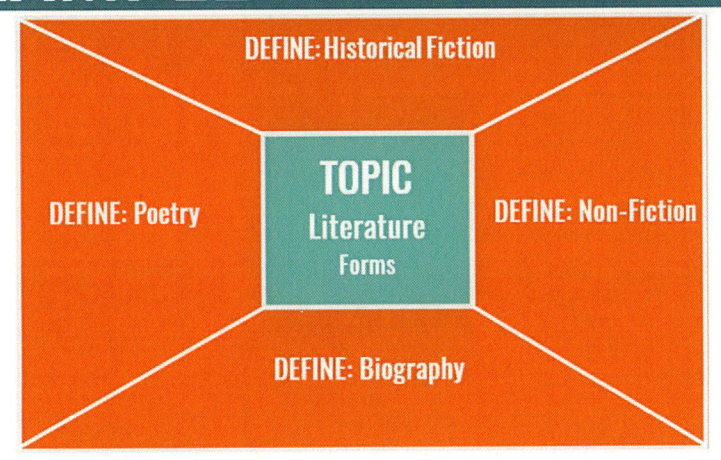

EXAMPLE

	DEFINE: Historical Fiction	
DEFINE: Poetry	**TOPIC** Literature Forms	DEFINE: Non-Fiction
	DEFINE: Biography	

HOT TIPS

• This strategy can also be done with movement and discussion. Students are asked a question and must go to the corner of the room labeled with their response. Students express their opinion and talk to others about why they have chosen that corner. This version of Four Corners promotes listening, verbal communication, critical thinking, and decision-making.

• Use the example organizer as a way for students to organize their thoughts independently and then have them go to their chosen corner to discuss.

© 2016, Stetson & Associates, Inc.

GALLERY WALK
Strategy 16

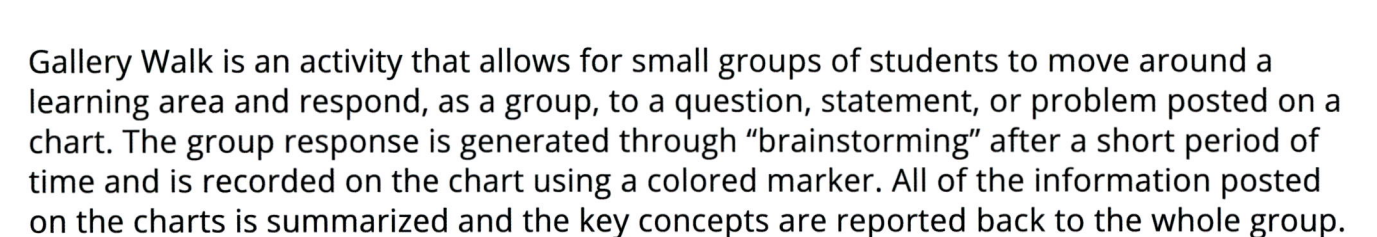

Gallery Walk is an activity that allows for small groups of students to move around a learning area and respond, as a group, to a question, statement, or problem posted on a chart. The group response is generated through "brainstorming" after a short period of time and is recorded on the chart using a colored marker. All of the information posted on the charts is summarized and the key concepts are reported back to the whole group.

HOT TIPS

- Use a different color marker for each group of students.

Gallery Walk:

- Provides opportunity for a focused review of key concepts.

- Allows for the application of the concepts previously taught.

- Allows for full participation of all students.

- Can be used as a pre-assessment, needs assessment, or post-assessment strategy.

- Allows for meaningful, scheduled movement for those students who have difficulty staying on task.

IMPLEMENTATION

1. Prepare a list of questions, statements, or problems.
2. Post the questions on charts along with a colored marker.
3. Group students using flexible grouping strategies.
4. Review the gallery walk procedures with the students.
5. Have each group select a recorder and assign a chart.
6. Give them 5 minutes to brainstorm responses at the first chart.
7. After 5 minutes, signal the students to move to the next chart.
8. After 3 minutes, signal the students to move again.
9. Continue the process in 3 minute intervals until the groups rotate through all charts.
10. Have all students return to their assigned seat except the recorder.
11. Have the recorder read the data and report the key concepts to the entire group.

EXAMPLE

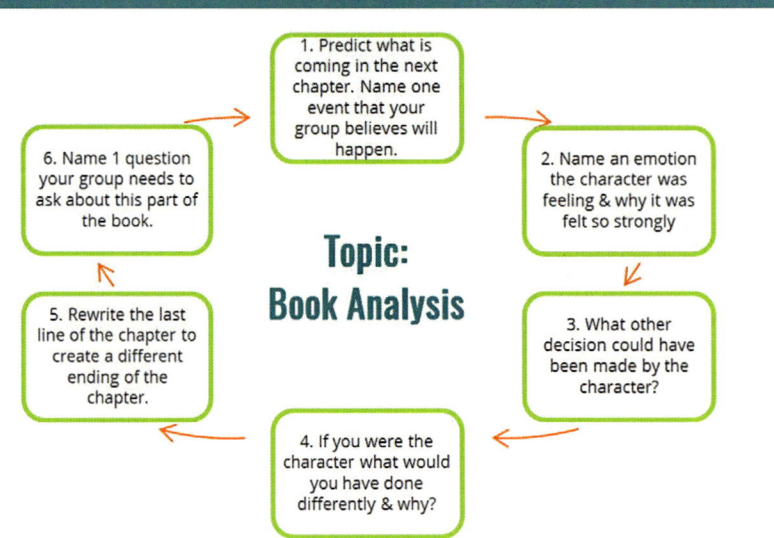

Topic: Book Analysis

1. Predict what is coming in the next chapter. Name one event that your group believes will happen.
2. Name an emotion the character was feeling & why it was felt so strongly
3. What other decision could have been made by the character?
4. If you were the character what would you have done differently & why?
5. Rewrite the last line of the chapter to create a different ending of the chapter.
6. Name 1 question your group needs to ask about this part of the book.

© 2016, Statson & Associates, Inc.

GIVE ONE-TAKE ONE
Strategy 17

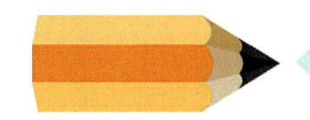

Give One-Take One is an active strategy that involves all students at the beginning of class to review homework or activate prior knowledge, during class to review information read/presented/discussed during the class, or at the end of class as a closure activity.

STUDENTS WHO BENEFIT:
- Experience difficulty maintaining attention, following ideas, or interpreting information presented orally.
- Need to get out of their seat and move purposefully in classroom.

IMPLEMENTATION

1. Students fold a piece of paper length-wise, open the paper and draw a line down the crease. On the left side of the page, they write "Give One" and number 1-3. On the right side of the page, write "Take One" and number 1-3.
2. Have students write the question or idea at the bottom of the paper. Provide think time and time to write three words, ideas or pictures that respond to the prompt on the "Give One" side.
3. Signal when to begin and students circulate to share with another classmate in pairs. The students "give one" of their items that is not on another student's list, and "take one" idea that is not on their own list. They thank the classmate and find a new partner.
4. Continue until each student has added three ideas to their list.
5. As each student completes their list, they are to move to the edge of the classroom and wait until others are finished.
6. For accountability, the teacher calls on students to share.

EXAMPLE

Give One…	Take One…
1.	1.
2.	2.
3.	3.

HOT TIPS

- Practice several times to ensure understanding of how to move around the classroom.
- Teach appropriate voice level.
- To signal who is done and lower the noise level, have students create a circle once they've completed their lists.
- Students may create a list using pictures, single words, or phrases depending upon their skills.

WHEN TO USE:

BEGINNING OF LESSON: Use to activate knowledge of previous lessons or to share homework.
DURING THE LESSON: Use to help students consolidate information, review what has just been discussed and provide a movement break, which will help to refocus attention.
AFTER LESSON: Use as review, closure or summarization of key concepts.

© 2016, Stetson & Associates, Inc.

GRAFFITI WALL
Strategy 18

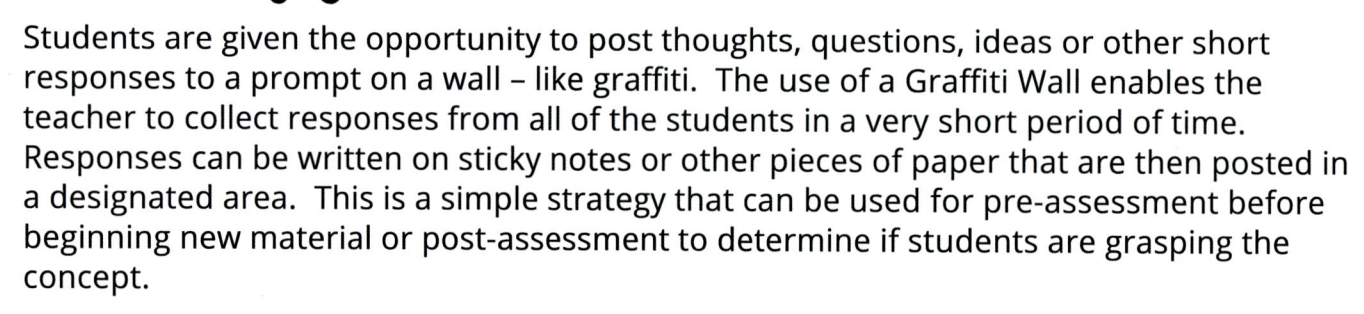

Students are given the opportunity to post thoughts, questions, ideas or other short responses to a prompt on a wall – like graffiti. The use of a Graffiti Wall enables the teacher to collect responses from all of the students in a very short period of time. Responses can be written on sticky notes or other pieces of paper that are then posted in a designated area. This is a simple strategy that can be used for pre-assessment before beginning new material or post-assessment to determine if students are grasping the concept.

HOT TIPS

- Remember to give think time.

- Consider technology. A Smart Board can make a great Graffiti Wall. Students can submit their responses electronically.

- Responses can be analyzed to inform further instruction.

- Allow students to group the responses.

- Leave the Graffiti Wall up during the lesson and check off the concepts/questions as they are addressed.

- Build in movement by letting students get up and post their responses.

IMPLEMENTATION

1. The teacher gives the cue or prompt to the class.

2. Allow a brief period of time for students to think about what they want to write.

3. At the teacher's signal, students post their response(s) on the Graffiti Wall.

4. Responses can then be analyzed to determine the level of understanding.

- Begin a new lesson by having students write down one thing they remember from yesterday's lesson to connect to prior learning.
- If attention is lagging, re-engage the class by having them write down one thing they just heard and place it on the graffiti wall.
- As students enter the room give them one sticky note and have them write a question they have about the instructional topic and place it on the Graffiti Wall.
- Use this strategy as a ticket out the door.

EXAMPLE

Graffiti Facts

Content, Concept or Skill:

What I KNOW?	What I Want to LEARN?	What I LEARNED?

Adapted from: *Differentiated Instruction: One Size Doesn't Fit All*, Gayle Gregory and Carolyn Chapman

© 2016, Stetson & Associates, Inc.

GRAPHIC ORGANIZERS
Strategy 19

Graphic organizers are visual representations (pictures, colors, words, and connectors) of content, that enable students to better process, remember, organize and demonstrate understanding.
- Assist visual and kinesthetic learners to better acquire and retain information.
- Can act as an alternative assessment tool for students who struggle with essay, short answer questions and forms of written output.
- Can act as an alternative method for note-taking.
- Serves as a "memory" mnemonic for remembering information.
- Teaches abstract concepts with more ease by offering a concrete representation.

IMPLEMENTATION

1. Describe the concept by discussion: the importance of organizing information, the various ways people organize information and the benefits of using a visual organizer.
2. Introduce a specific graphic organizer by describing its purpose.
3. Explain and demonstrate the use of the selected organizer with familiar information and then with new content.
4. Let students apply the organizer to familiar information, then to relatively easy new material.
5. Have students reflect on the use of the graphic organizer by sharing their examples and evaluating the effectiveness.
6. Provide multiple opportunities for students to practice.
7. Encourage students to construct their own organizers.

HOT TIPS

- Explicitly teach students by modeling.

- Organizers can be global or very detailed.

- Organizers are typically a one-page form with blank areas or shapes for the student to fill in with related information.

- Organizers should increase in complexity as the subject matter becomes more complex.

- Encourage students to complete the organizer with pictures, words and/or simple connectors that illustrate the relationship of the various parts.

EXAMPLE

1. Descriptive
2. Time Sequence
3. Process/Cause Effect
4. Episode
5. Generalization/Principle
6. Concept

© 2016, Stetson & Associates, Inc.

HIGHLIGHTED TEXT
Strategy 20

When highlighting texts, students are making key points visually prominent. It is important to teach students what to highlight since highlighting everything in a paragraph can be more of a hindrance than a benefit.

HOT TIPS

• After you have highlighted one or two textbook chapters or other print materials, sit with the student and ask if this approach is helpful.

• Ask how you might adapt your highlighting of the text to make it easier for the student to learn and remember the content.

• After receiving this feedback, you will want to make any adjustments that seem appropriate.

• Remember this is a resource for the student, so your own personal preference or learning style is not the key to success in highlighting materials.

IMPLEMENTATION

1. Be sure you are allowed to mark in the textbook or supplemental materials before you begin.
2. Scan the chapter or material before highlighting to be sure that you can identify the main ideas throughout the text.
3. Highlight key points in yellow.
4. Highlight key terminology and their definitions if available in another color, such as pink or green.
5. The main idea of each paragraph is usually contained in the first sentence but it can sometimes be found elsewhere in the paragraph, such as the ending sentence. Beside each main idea, consider writing the notation (MI) or put an asterisk or other marking.
6. If there is a chart or important graphic, also mark in yellow to illustrate the main idea or point of the information contained there.
7. Consider creating a one-page print version of the main ideas and key vocabulary words that the student can use to study in preparation for studying and/or for testing.

EXAMPLE

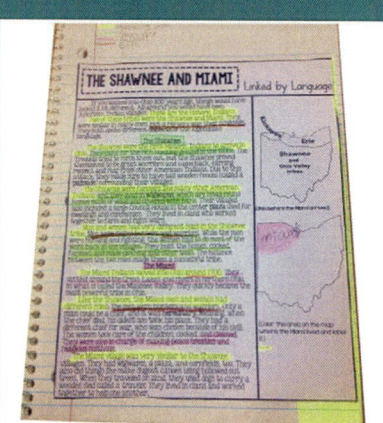

Use more than one color!

Be selective!

Use online highlighting tools to highlight and annotate on the computer or tablet!

Photo Credit: www.wherethewildthingslearn.com

© 2016, Stetson & Associates, Inc.

INSIDE-OUTSIDE CIRCLES
Strategy 21

Inside-Outside Circles are an alternative to oral reports and board work where the majority of students sit passively. This strategy allows students to respond to questions and discuss a variety of topics with several peers in an organized manner.

IMPLEMENTATION

1. In one variation, the teacher fdivides the class into two large groups. One group forms an inner circle, seated with their backs to the inside, facing outward. The other forms an outer circle facing in, with each student seated facing a member of the inner circle.
2. The teacher introduces a problem, asks a question, or invites an opinion.
3. Each pair discusses the question, helps each other solve the problem, or listens as the members of each pair make brief presentations on a topic they have prepared or thought up on the spot.
4. The teacher monitors each round carefully and directs the students in the outer circle to move one seat in a clockwise direction so that they are seated across from a new partner. This process continues until the teachers ends it.

EXAMPLE

Watch it in action!

www.theteachertoolkit.com/index.php/tool/inside-outside-circles

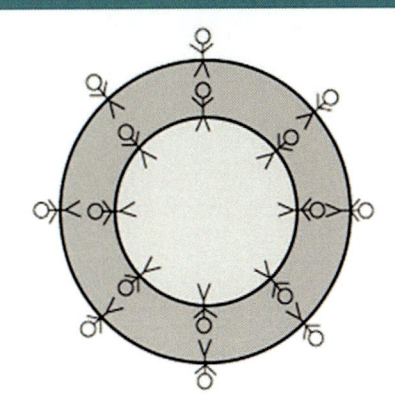

Source: Teacher Education Resources
P.O. Box 13747   Gainesville, Florida 32609   1-800-617-2100

© 2016, Stetson & Associates, Inc.

HOT TIPS

- The circles activity can also work with pairs, trios, or small groups forming inner and outer circles facing each other. The members of one pair, small group, etc., make a presentation or report to the members of a similar sized group in the other circle. The members of the listening group then respond, saying what they liked about the presentation, or agreeing or disagreeing with an answer to a problem, and so forth. Then the other small group takes its turn, and gets feedback from the group across from them.

- Kagan suggests pulling the groups out of the circle, and give them time to improve their presentation.

INTERACTIVE NOTEBOOKS
Strategy 22

An interactive notebook is a student-writing booklet (typically spiral) that enables the learner to take notes, record learning AND express ideas in a creative, interactive format. Use of this practice promotes independent thinkers and writers to acquire rich knowledge and understanding.

HOT TIPS

- Use a rubric to grade and assess the components.

- Have creative materials available for the students to use (glue, colored pencils, scissors, magazines, etc.).

- Establish procedures for use of the notebooks including do's and don'ts.

- Provide examples and positive feedback to the students.

- Search for "Images of Interactive Notebooks-Google 100+pictures" online.

- Have students critique each other's entries once a level of trust and comfort is established.

IMPLEMENTATION

1. Encourage students to create a colorful front cover using drawings, magazines, personal photos and other creative items that represent the subject area. Have the student attach a manila envelope on the inside of the back cover to keep Works in Progress.
2. Have students prepare an Author Page in the inside front cover that reflects who they are using pictures, illustrations and written descriptions.
3. Use the next 2-3 pages as the Table of Contents. Here the student will record the entries with the corresponding page numbers. Have them number the remaining pages in the notebook.
4. Instruct students to use the RIGHT side of the notebook to record lecture notes, handout notes, discussion notes, graphic organizers, etc. This is the COMMON set of information provided typically by the teacher or resource such as textbook, videos, internet, etc.
5. Direct the students to use the LEFT side of the notebook to PROCESS new ideas using flowcharts, illustrations, diagrams, poetry, colors, cartoons, etc. For a complete list go to upstagereview.org.

EXAMPLES   Adapted from: History Alive

- Cartoon or comic strips
- Maps
- Slide sketches
- Book Covers or CD Covers
- Eulogies
- Facial Expressions
- Caricatures
- Flow Charts
- Illustrated Dictionary
- Timelines
- Postcards or Posters
- Mind Notes
- Mosaics
- Sensory Figures
- Advertisements
- Venn/Spoke Diagrams
- T-Charts
- Pictowords
- "What If" statements
- Invitations

© 2016, Stetson & Associates, Inc.

JIGSAW
Strategy 23

Jigsaw is an activity that allows for students to work in small groups, yet cover a body of information on different topics. Students meet initially in "Home Groups" to review previously introduced content. They separate into "Expert Groups" for a specified amount of time for in-depth study on a topic. The students then return to their original "Home Group" and teach the other group members the essential information from the topic.

IMPLEMENTATION

1. Assign 5-7 students to Home Groups based upon flexible grouping strategies.
2. Establish the group work norms with the students.
3. Establish transitioning procedures with the groups.
4. Each member of the Home Group numbers off from 1 to 5.
5. Students read their Expert Group assignment individually. All the 1s will read the same content, 2s the same, etc.
6. Students move to their Expert Group (all the 1s, 2s, etc.)
7. The Expert Group plans a 3-5 minute "teaching segment" of the reading material they have discussed. All students will do the same Expert Group presentation when they return to their Home Group.
8. After a specified period of time, have the Experts move back to their Home Group and teach their peers the content.

HOT TIPS

• Enables all students to participate in the learning experience.

• Allows for a large body of work to be covered because rather than each student reading 7 pieces of information, they become experts on one topic.

• The struggling reader is exposed to all of the content without having to read all of the information.

• Provides opportunities for purposeful movement for students who may have difficulty staying on task.

• Increases students' retention by allowing them to teach others and use the information immediately.

EXAMPLE

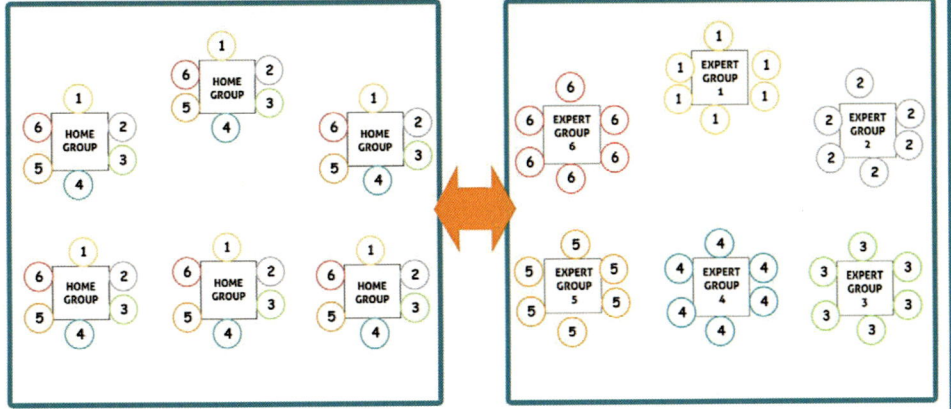

© 2016, Stetson & Associates, Inc.

LITTLE FOLDABLE BOOKLET
Strategy 24

Foldable Booklet is a pre-assessment strategy that gives students an opportunity to share what they know about a given topic within a set of guiding questions.

Source for Fold: Dinah Zike's Stapleless Poof Book

HOT TIPS

Variations for this pre-assessing activity may include:

- Allow students to pair up with one another.

- Groups can consolidate ideas to expand responses.

- A few examples may be given to trigger student brainstorm.

- Have some premade booklets available for students who may struggle with the folding and cutting.

- Instead of cutting with scissors, students may tear the fold in step 3 and 4.

IMPLEMENTATION

1. Predetermine the question or task for each page of the booklet.

2. State the purpose of the strategy. Show an example of the final product of this foldable.

3. Model the folding directions for the booklet. Allow for students to complete this part of the activity before moving to the next step.

4. List the question for each page (Definition, Key Vocabulary & Examples)

5. Select the best method to record student knowledge (paper/pencil, oral explanation, drawing pictures, computer software, etc.).

6. Allow approximately 10 minutes.

EXAMPLE Adapted from: History Alive

1. FOLD
2. FOLD / FOLD / FOLD
3. CUT
4. FOLD
5. PULL APART
6. PUSH TOGETHER
7. FOLD
8. FOLD

© 2016, Stetson & Associates, Inc.

MINDSTREAMING
Strategy 25

The Mindstreaming strategy enhances clarifying, summarizing and paraphrasing skills for students as they process new content and information. Mindstreaming actively involves students by requiring them to "stream" their understanding by talking about what they know (or think they know) while focusing on the content. This strategy can also be used as a quick break activity during a lesson to allow students a chance to reflect on what they just learned.

Adapted from: Buehl, 1995, Santa, C., Havens, L. and B. Valdes, 2004.

IMPLEMENTATION

1. Pair students by identifying Partner A and Partner B.
2. Identify the topic to be discussed.
3. Partner A talks for one minute about the assigned topic. Partner B only listens, nodding and encouraging non-verbally. It is okay if Partner A repeats himself, as repeating sometimes jogs the memory.
4. After the teacher calls one minute, the partners switch roles. Now, Partner B shares and Partner A listens and non-verbally encourages Partner B.

OPTIONAL:
Repeat the process for 40 seconds and then 20 seconds to continue the review.

5. After completing the group discussion format, bring the class back together and summarize what was discussed in the groups.

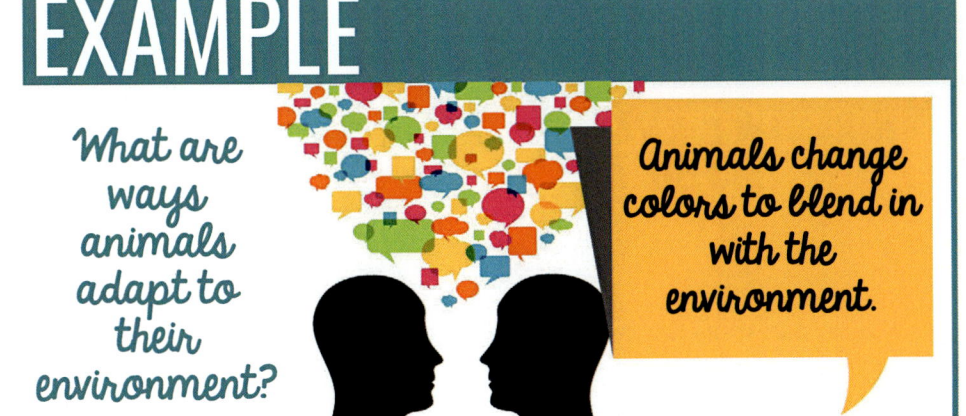

HOT TIPS

- Use to activate prior knowledge, discuss a new topic or summarize what has been read or learned.
- Make sure to encourage partners to not repeat anything stated by their partner.
- Fast paced strategy that allows students to summarize information.
- Time periods can be modified to fit the needs of students.
- Begin with 15-30 second time period, then increase time period to 60 seconds.
- Accommodate by allowing students to use notes or textbooks.
- First, teach the process with a concept students know well, such as a movie, television show, sports or music. Once students understand the process, then embed the content.

EXAMPLE

What are ways animals adapt to their environment?

Animals change colors to blend in with the environment.

© 2016, Stetson & Associates, Inc.

MIX & MINGLE
Strategy 26

This is a strategy for previewing text and making predictions. Students are given short excerpts from a text and mingle with their peers to look at the different phrases and make predictions about the elements of the text that is getting ready to be read.

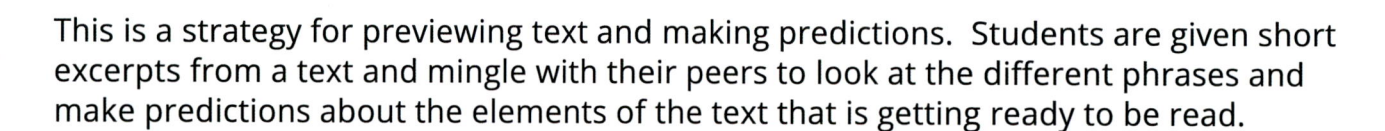

Adapted from Beers, G. K. (2003). When kids can't read, what teachers can do: A guide for teachers, 6-12.

HOT TIPS

- Make copies of pictures in the book for pre-readers.

- Model the process the first time it's used.

- Use sentences/phrases exactly as they exist in the book without paraphrasing.

- Students can mingle with the whole class or they could mingle within a smaller subset of the class.

IMPLEMENTATION

1. Select short words, sentences or phrases from the book or other text that is going to be read.
2. Prepare strips of paper or index cards with one of the words, sentences or phrases on each strip or card. Have enough copies so that each student gets one.
3. Pass out the cards making sure that each student has one.
4. At your signal, the students find a partner and mingle. Student A reads their phrase and then Student B reads theirs. The partners then ask, "What's this story about?".
5. At your signal the students find another partner and repeat the process. Students continue changing partners, mixing and mingling until the teacher tells them to stop.
6. Debriefing can be conducted in many ways. This can be done in small groups, partners, or by leading the whole group in a discussion allowing the students to make predictions about the text.
7. Read the text and let the group check their prediction accuracy.

EXAMPLE

- Have students mix and mingle before beginning a new story in ELA.

- Place math vocabulary words on the cards to reintroduce the terms before starting a unit on fractions.

- Use this strategy to preview content that will be viewed on an instructional video about U. S. History.

© 2016, Stetson & Associates, Inc.

MOTIVATIONAL MENTOR
Strategy 27

Students work with a partner to solve problems or answer questions. One student is the worker while the other partner is the mentor. The mentor gives direction, explanation and encouragement while teaching the worker how to solve the problem. Partners trade roles so that each person gets a chance to be the mentor and each person gets the chance to be the worker.

Adapted from Kagan's Rally Coach

IMPLEMENTATION

1. Students are put into groups of two with one student identified as the mentor and one as the worker.

2. Give the groups a question or problem to solve.

3. The mentor teaches the worker how to solve the problem. The mentor checks work, gives encouragement, and provides instruction if necessary. The worker is the one with the pencil solving the problem.

4. Trade roles and present another question.

EXAMPLES

In Math, one student mentors the other while they solve word problems. Partners trade roles after every problem.

In Science, one student conducts the experiment while their mentor monitors and gives feedback.

One student spells their vocabulary words while the other student listens, gives feedback and records responses.

HOT TIPS

- Define the roles and practice before using this strategy for the first time. Share several examples of how to verbally mentor another student such as "I really like how you are doing…" and "What if you tried…"
- Monitor the guidance that is being given by the partners to make sure they are not just giving the correct answer.
- Consider how students are placed with partners. There could be some students who would not work together well.
- Make sure that the mentor has the correct answer by providing a key. This ensures they are "mentoring" their partner to the correct response.
- This strategy works for questions that have one correct answer.

ONE-SENTENCE SUMMARY
Strategy 28

There are different levels of summarization, from a thorough summarization of a main idea and supporting details to a one or two word summarization. One-Sentence Summary falls between the two extremes. Using this strategy, students summarize the main idea and vital details in one sentence. Students transform information to make it their own. This brief writing indicates the student's level of understanding, involves the student in interacting with the content, and provides the teacher with feedback regarding student comprehension.

Adapted from: Comprehension Shouldn't be Silent and Creating Independence Through Student-Owned Strategies

HOT TIPS

- To encourage brevity, provide students with an index card or sticky note.
- Complete orally, use as a journal entry, or write on a note card.
- Use to summarize, describe, sequence, compare and contrast and/or show problem-solution relationships.
- Use after presentations, videos, online research or field trips.
- Can be completed alone, in pairs or small groups.
- Combine 3-4 one-sentence summaries into a paragraph.

BEFORE: Activate prior knowledge, review a concept previously taught or as a pre-assessment
DURING: Check for understanding
AFTER: Closure activity at end of lesson or class period to help students synthesize and summarize concepts

IMPLEMENTATION

1. Explicitly teach students how to utilize the One-Sentence Summary frame, modeling how to summarize using content familiar to the student. Teach one sentence type at a time, putting the sentence template on a sentence strip or chart.
2. Read the text, then model selecting one of the sentence frames and summarizing the information. For some students, you may need to tell them which sentence frame to utilize, while other students can select their own.
3. Write summaries as a whole class; provide many examples and opportunities for practice prior to having students complete the summaries independently.

EXAMPLE

Description
A _____ is a kind of _____ that _____.

Sequence
_____ begins with _____, continues with _____ and ends with _____.

Compare and Contrast
_____ and _____ are similar in that both _____, but _____ while _____.

Cause and Effect
_____ causes _____.

Problem and Solution
_____ wanted _____ but _____ so _____.

A fairy tale is a kind of story that is make believe; there is magic and the animals talk.
Three Little Pigs begins with the pigs leaving home to seek their fortune, continues with the wolf blowing down two of the houses, and ends with the pig in the brick house living happily ever after.
The Little Pigs and The True Story of the Three Little Pigs are similar in that both are about three little pigs and a wolf, but one story is from the pigs' point of view and the other is from the wolf's perspective.

© 2016, Stetson & Associates, Inc.

POP QUIZ SWAP
Strategy 29

In this strategy students quiz each other on a topic that is given to them. Students will have an opportunity to work with multiple classmates as they keep swapping partners, quizzing each other, and swapping prompt cards until the time is up for the activity.

Adapted from Kagan's Quiz-Quiz-Trade Activity

IMPLEMENTATION

1. Give each student a card with a question and the correct answer on it.

2. Have students pair up with their shoulder partner.

3. Student A reads the question on their card and Student B guesses the correct answer. Student A can give clues if the first attempt is incorrect.

4. Student B reads the prompt on their card and Student A guesses the correct answer.

5. When both partners have figured out the correct answer they swap cards and find new partners.

6. Students continue pop quizzing and swapping until the teacher signals that time has expired.

EXAMPLES

- In Math, have a problem on one side of a card and the correct answer on the other side. Partners have to solve the problem.

- Have a vocabulary word on one side of a card and the definition on the other. Partners have to give the correct definition.

- Place all of the vocabulary (or spelling) words on a word wall. Place the definitions on the cards. Partners identify the correct word based on its definition.

HOT TIPS

- Model the strategy the first time it is used.

- Communicate your expectations about voice level before beginning since there will be a lot of people talking at the same time.

- Use a visual timer and/or music to cue the students when time is up.

- Actively monitor students, as they are moving about the room.

- Teach students how to cue their partner if they get the answer wrong.

PORTFOLIO ASSESSMENT
Strategy 30

Portfolio assessment is a differentiated assessment strategy where individual student work samples are gathered over time for the purpose of demonstrating student skills, interests, learning styles, and progress and/or mastery of learning. The portfolio process promotes self-directed learners and enables collaboration between the teacher and learners.

HOT TIPS

- Portfolios can be any type of container such as a pizza box, pocket file, and/or notebook. Be sure the container can hold the variety of samples that will be gathered.

- Don't forget to date each item and code the selected item.

- Attach a "table of contents" sheet to the portfolio to document items selected.

- Having a portfolio encourages student ownership of learning and reflection of progress. It also provides opportunity for dialogue between teacher and learners.

IMPLEMENTATION

1. Form a partnership with the learner and determine the criteria for the student work samples.
2. Gather work samples based upon the criteria. Work samples can include but are not limited to homework, projects, group reports, videos, audio recordings, written pieces, lists of books read, mind maps, graphic organizers, tests, peer reviews, photographs, and/or computer generated presentations.
3. The teacher and student choose items to be placed in the portfolio.
4. The student writes and attaches an analysis of the item selected, telling why this work sample was chosen and what criteria it satisfies.
5. The student reviews the collection and sets goals for future learning in a collaborative manner with the teacher. The teacher then notes areas of strength, where improvement is needed and helps the student set future goals.
6. The student holds a portfolio conference with the teacher and possibly the parents.

EXAMPLE

PORTFOLIO ASSESSMENT DOCUMENTATION

Contents	Selection	Reflection	Comments

© 2016, Stetson & Associates, Inc.

PRE-TEACHING VOCABULARY
Strategy 31

Effective vocabulary instruction includes multiple exposures using varying definitions. This allows students to create understanding of the relationships between and among words in order to recognize and create novel contexts. General and special educators collaborate regularly to identify key vocabulary for the coming week. The special educator may pull the student at either the end of the week or the beginning of the week to do a preteach to "front load" those words for the student.

IMPLEMENTATION

1. Both teachers agree on a system of collaborating to identify key vocabulary to be introduced in the coming week. It's important to set a time and a place for when this will happen. Depending upon the level of the student, the list may include only the most important words/terms.

2. The special educator works with the student to identify a time in his/her schedule when it is convenient to pull the student for a 30-minute session.

3. Select appropriate vocabulary strategies and work with the student to explore the new terms.

HOT TIPS

- Focus on about 10 words/terms each week.

- The vocabulary strategy used will become a support and a study guide for the student in class.

- As the student becomes proficient with the strategies, have them complete the work independently for some words and then discuss with you.

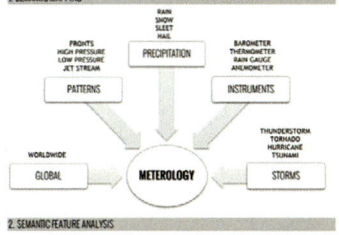

EXAMPLES

1. SEMANTIC MAPPING

2. SEMANTIC FEATURE ANALYSIS

	ELECTED	DICTATORSHIP	MULTI-PARTY	MAJORITY RULE	PRIVATE OWNERSHIP	INDIVIDUAL FREEDOM
Democracy						
Communism						
Socialism						
Fascism						
Tribal Rule						

2. SEMANTIC FEATURE ANALYSIS

	ELECTED	DICTATORSHIP	MULTI-PARTY	MAJORITY RULE	PRIVATE OWNERSHIP	INDIVIDUAL FREEDOM
Democracy						
Communism						
Socialism						
Fascism						
Tribal Rule						

3. DESCRIBING HIERARCHY

a) NAME:	The students state the name of the object that is to be described.
b) CATEGORY:	The students state the category in which the object belongs.
c) FUNCTION:	The students state the use of the object.
d) ATTRIBUTES:	The students state the physical properties of the object.

Example #1
a) Tyrannosaurus
b) Tyrannosaurus is a dinosaur
c) Tyrannosaurus was a carnivorous scavenger
d) Tyrannosaurus was the largest carnivorous dinosaur. It had a huge neck, strong jaw muscles, sharp teeth and a long tail

Example #2
a) Microscope
b) A microscope is an optical instrument
c) A microscope allows you to magnify very small objects so they can be seen
d) A microscope consists of a lens or combination of lenses with an eyepiece and a platform for placing the object to be viewed

4. DEFINITION MAP

NAME	WHAT IS IT?	WHAT IS IT LIKE?	EXAMPLES	NON-EXAMPLES
Percussion	Musical instrument	Sound is produced when it is struck. Can be made from wood, skin, metal, etc.	Drums, symbols, bells, tambourine, xylophone	Flute, violin, trumpet, clarinet

© 2016, Stetson & Associates, Inc.

PREVIEWING
Strategy 32

Previewing allows students to become familiar with content and anticipate the meaning or purpose of the text or lesson. This strategy supports students who have difficulty reading or comprehending text by activating prior knowledge and creating a framework for learning.

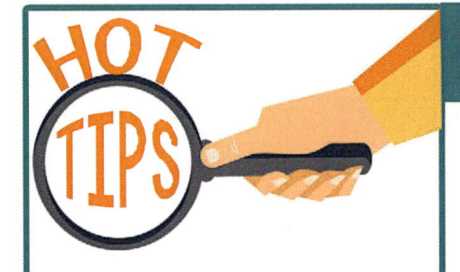

HOT TIPS

- Foster independent development of this practice by routine use with new texts.

- Use at the beginning of the lesson to activate prior knowledge.

- Previewing can be combined with a graphic organizer or concept map to provide a framework for learning and comprehension.

- Introduce this strategy to students by asking them if they have seen the previews for movies. Ask what they learn from those previews, why they watch the previews, etc.

IMPLEMENTATION

1. Read the title.

2. Read the headings and subheadings.

3. Notice visual aids (maps, diagrams, photographs, charts or graphs).

4. Examine vocabulary words in bold or italic print.

5. Ask the following questions:
   - What does this text seem to be about?
   - What do I already know about this story/subject?
   - What do the subheadings tell me about the topic?
   - What kind of text is this?
   - What do the highlighted words/phrases tell me?
   - What clues do the visual aids give me about the text?
   - How is the information organized?

EXAMPLE

EXAMPLE: Becoming THIEVES

T	Title
H	Headings
I	Introduction
E	Every first sentence in a paragraph
V	Visuals and Vocabulary
E	End of chapter questions
S	Summary

© 2016, Stetson & Associates, Inc.

PROMPT SEQUENCE
Strategy 33

Prompts and cues are tools used to assist a student in completing a task by allowing them to be as independent as possible. In the prompt sequence, assistance is given in the smallest amount appropriate to meet the needs of the student. More intrusive levels of prompts are not used unless lower levels of support have not been successful. Following the prompt sequence teaches the student to be as independent as possible and encourages errorless learning because the student is prompted to be successful at the task every time.

IMPLEMENTATION

PRE-ASSESSMENT
1. Give the student a task to complete.

2. Observe to see which parts of the task the student completes independently.

INSTRUCTION
3. If the student is not successful, give a gestural prompt.

4. If the student is still not successful, give a verbal prompt.

5. Continue through the prompt sequence if necessary to support the student toward successful completion of the task.

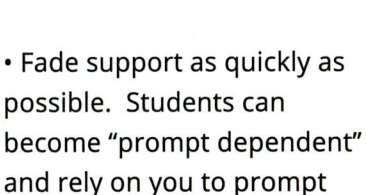

EXAMPLE

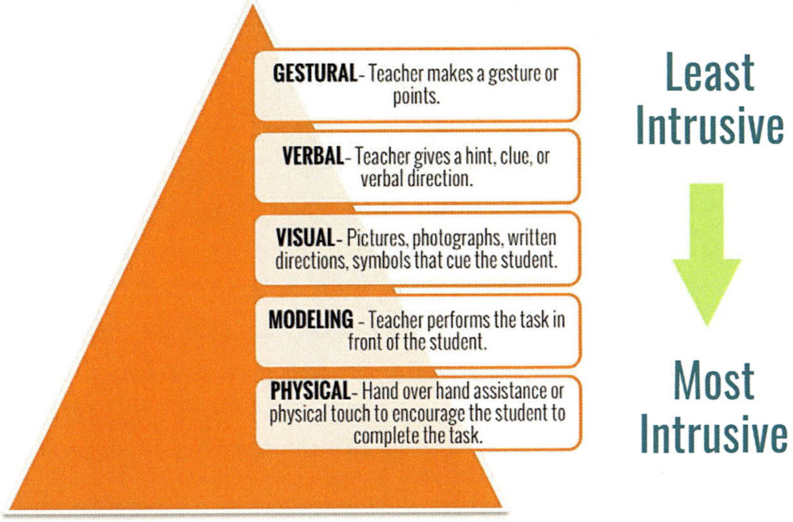

GESTURAL - Teacher makes a gesture or points.

VERBAL - Teacher gives a hint, clue, or verbal direction.

VISUAL - Pictures, photographs, written directions, symbols that cue the student.

MODELING - Teacher performs the task in front of the student.

PHYSICAL - Hand over hand assistance or physical touch to encourage the student to complete the task.

Least Intrusive → Most Intrusive

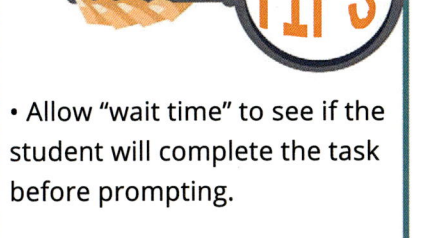

HOT TIPS

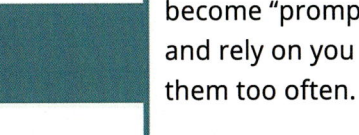

- Allow "wait time" to see if the student will complete the task before prompting.

- Keep documentation to show the level of support the student needs.

- Fade support as quickly as possible. Students can become "prompt dependent" and rely on you to prompt them too often.

- Don't assume that students need the same level of support every day. Give them a chance to perform the task with little or no prompting.

Q&A CONSENSUS
Strategy 34

The Q&A Consensus strategy is a great cooperative learning activity that allows each student to participate and be held accountable for learning the material. This strategy is often used to review material that has already been taught.

Adapted from Kagan's Numbered Heads Together Strategy
Kagan, S. (1989). "The structural approach to cooperative learning." Educational Leadership. 47(4): p. 12-15.

HOT TIPS

- The question asked can be either low level recall, right answer questions, or high-level analysis and evaluation questions or problems. Use question stems to help students write quality questions!

- If there is more than one answer to a question the teacher can have multiple students from the selected number group answer.

- Often an assessment is given after Q&A Consensus is played.

- Final group responses to each question can be recorded in a collaborative online document such as a Google Doc so there is a comprehensive study sheet once the game has ended.

IMPLEMENTATION

1. After studying a topic, students write one question or problem pertaining to the lesson using prior knowledge of how to write higher-level questions.
2. Students write their question on a sticky note and add it to a chart hanging in the classroom.
3. Once all questions are collected, the teacher selects five to ask the class. Each student has time to think about and/or write down their response to each question.
4. Students are divided into five groups and assigned numbers. If the groups are uneven, numbers can be duplicated. Each group is given a sticky note with one of the five questions.
5. During a designated time period (ex. 3 minutes) students discuss their answers to the first question and come to a group consensus.
6. Rotate the sticky note questions between groups and the discussion process begins again. This continues until each group has had a chance to discuss and agree upon an answer to all five questions.
7. The teacher then calls a number to identify a group member to be the spokesperson for the group. The teacher selects one student to share the consensus answer to one of the questions. This is repeated until all questions have been discussed.

EXAMPLE

If a class clicker response system, chromebooks, tablets, cell phones, etc. are available, have students answer using technology. This is an appropriate way to use technology in the classroom to engage students!

© 2016, Stetson & Associates, Inc.

RAFT
Strategy 35

RAFT is a writing strategy that can be applied to any content area and works well with all grade levels. This activity can be differentiated for gifted or struggling learners. It provides student choice and allows students to be grouped by interests and strengths. This engaging activity allows students to demonstrate learning while being creative.

Example adapted from: Differentiated Instruction in the Foreign Language Classroom: Meeting the Diverse Needs of all Learners. Toni Theisen, Loveland, Co. The Communiqué PDF: Page 4.

IMPLEMENTATION

1. Select an area of study currently taking place in your classroom.
2. Model how to complete a RAFT with the students' assistance. Allow them to help select the role, audience, format and topic.
3. Give students another writing prompt with a preselected role, audience, format, and topic. Allow the students to complete a RAFT independently. When they are finished, have a couple students share aloud and discuss the differences and similarities.
4. When students are comfortable provide a chart of options for each category. Eventually, they can select any RAFT to write about.

R: Students choose the ROLE of the writer.

A: Students select the AUDIENCE to address.

F: Students decide on a FORMAT for the writing.

T: Students pick a TOPIC to write about.

HOT TIPS

- Ensure that your RAFT appeals to a broad range of student interests, learner profiles, and readiness levels.

- Differentiate your RAFT through content, process, product, and/or environment.

- By using this strategy, teachers encourage students to write creatively, consider a topic from multiple perspectives, and gain the ability to write for different audiences.

EXAMPLE

Role	Audience	Format	Topic
Customer	Hotel Employee	Letter	Make a reservation for several nights. Include all details.
Hotel Employee	Customer	Reply Letter	Confirm reservation details. Include changes.
Customer	Hotel Manager	Complaint	Demand compensation for problems and poor service.
Parisian Real Estate Agency	Prospective Renters	Real Estate Ad.	Describe details of the apartments available for rent.
Students who want to study abroad	Study abroad organization	Application form for the program	Apply for a rigorous study abroad program.
Students who stayed with a family	Family Members	Thank you note	Thank the family for the home stay and tell them about your return trip.

© 2016, Stetson & Associates, Inc.

RESPONSE CARDS
Strategy 36

Response cards are pre-printed, write-on or student-made cards that are held up simultaneously by all students. They display responses to questions or problems presented by the teacher. Response cards may contain pictures and/or words that are content specific (i.e., science terms, mathematical operations, grammar) or they can contain generic symbols (yes/no, agree/disagree). Response cards may also consist of a blank writing surface, whereby students write their responses.

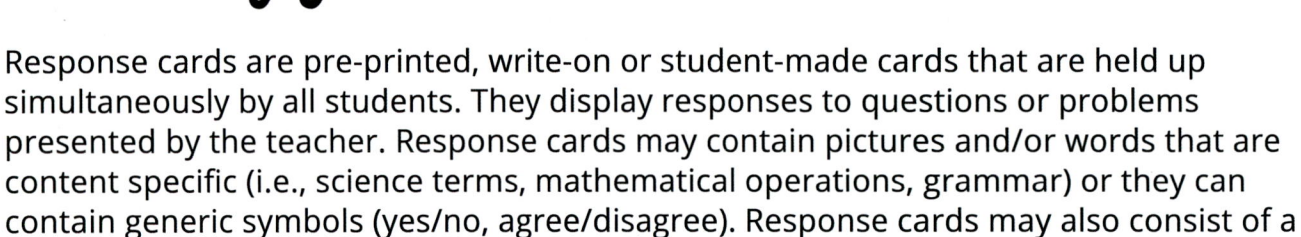

HOT TIPS

• Enables every student to respond, reducing passive participation or day dreaming.

• Assists teachers in ongoing monitoring of student progress.

• Allows students to learn from one another.

• Are highly motivating and add an element of fun.

• Provides for wait or think time before accepting answers.

• Increases on task behavior.

• Increases overall learning.

• Provides for a differentiated product or assessment of learning.

IMPLEMENTATION

1. Determine the type of response cards based on the instructional delivery. A few examples are yes/no, content-specific or student write-on cards.
2. Instruct students on the acceptable procedures for using response cards – where to hold the card, how to point to a response, etc.
3. Deliver instruction to students.
4. Elicit responses from students.
5. Note responses either formally (written documentation) or informally (observation).
6. Move to the next teaching interaction or re-teach, based on the responses provided by the students.
7. Make written or mental notes of students who are struggling with the content. These students could become a flexible group for small group instruction.

EXAMPLE

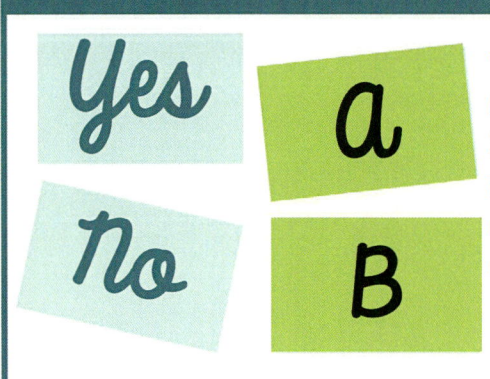

Yes / No

a / B

"If response cards were used instead of hand raising for just 30 minutes per day, each student would make more than 3,700 additional academic responses during the school year."
~Heward et al, 1996.

© 2016, Stetson & Associates, Inc.

ROUND ROBIN
Strategy 37

This cooperative learning activity is an excellent technique for actively involving students in the learning process. It can be utilized to share or review information, improve communication skills, and improve students' interpersonal skills.

IMPLEMENTATION

1. Students are divided into small groups of 4-6 students and one person is chosen to be the scribe.

2. Teacher provides the topic of conversation or the problem to be discussed. This question should have several different answers.

3. Allow students a designated amount of time to think independently about the answer. Use a timer.

4. Students take turns sharing out loud, rotating around the group in a clockwise circle. The scribe records all of the answers.

EXTENSION: If you assign a different question to each group, the recorded answer pages can be rotated between groups and students repeat the Round Robin process to add new answers to the page. They may not repeat any answers already provided by students in other groups.

EXAMPLE

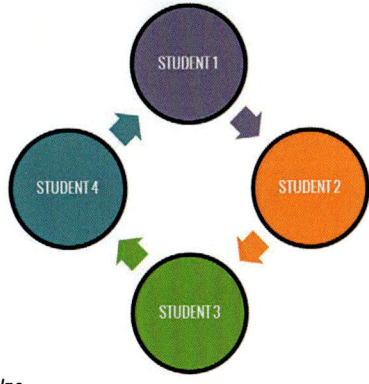

- STUDENT 1
- STUDENT 2
- STUDENT 3
- STUDENT 4

HOT TIPS

- This strategy can be utilized at the beginning of a lesson, as an anticipatory component or to activate prior knowledge.

- This strategy can be utilized during the lesson to check for understanding, as a closure or summary at the end of a lesson.

- Remind students to use their three-inch voices in order to control noise level. Demonstrate this ahead of time with a model group.

- Consider using a timer to encourage equal sharing time if you notice a problem.

RUBRICS
Strategy 38

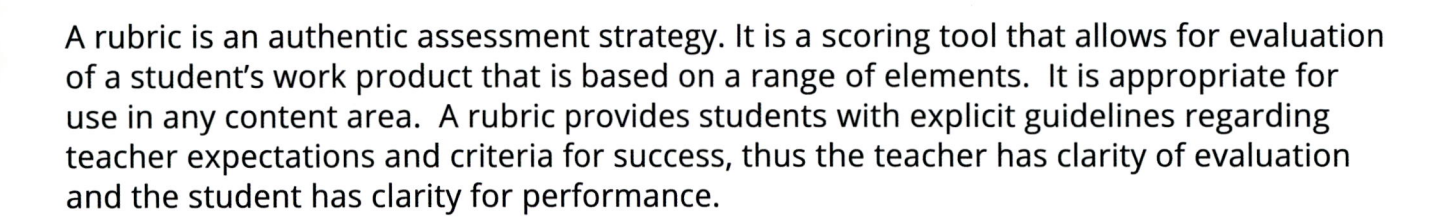

A rubric is an authentic assessment strategy. It is a scoring tool that allows for evaluation of a student's work product that is based on a range of elements. It is appropriate for use in any content area. A rubric provides students with explicit guidelines regarding teacher expectations and criteria for success, thus the teacher has clarity of evaluation and the student has clarity for performance.

HOT TIPS

- Assign different weights to different aspects of the elements to determine a numerical grade.

- Use the rubric as a dialogue tool between teacher and learner.

- Students can use rubrics as a tool to develop skills.

- Rubrics provide the teacher a means to offer necessary scaffolding.

- Rubrics encourage student ownership and increase learning.

IMPLEMENTATION

1. Determine the concept and the essential learning objective(s).

2. Choose the criteria and evidence to be produced.

3. Develop a grid and apply the concept and criteria.

4. Share the rubric with the student when assigning the task.

5. Evaluate the final product.

EXAMPLE

EXAMPLE: Pepperoni Pizza
Elements for Judgment: # of pepperoni slices, texture, color and taste

RANK 4: DELICIOUS	RANK 3: GOOD
• Pepperoni in every bite • Chewy • Golden crust with melted cheese • Home-baked taste	• Pepperoni in 75% of bites • Chewy in middle, crispy on edges • Brown from over-cooking or light from undercooking • Quality store-bought taste
RANK 2: NEEDS IMPROVEMENT	**RANK 1: POOR**
• Pepperoni in 50% of bites • Texture crispy from over-cooking • Either dark brown or light • Tasteless, low-fat content	• Too few/too many pepperoni slices • Texture resembles cardboard • Burned • Store-bought flavor with freezer burn

	4: DELICIOUS	3: GOOD	2: NI	1: POOR
# Pepperonis	Every bite			
Texture	Chewy			
Color	Golden			
Taste	Home-Baked			

© 2016, Stetson & Associates, Inc.

SELECTIVE HIGHLIGHTING
Strategy 39

Selective highlighting is used to help students organize what they have read by selecting what is important. This strategy teaches students to highlight ONLY the key words, phrases, vocabulary and ideas that are central to understanding the reading.

IMPLEMENTATION

1. Introduce students to the selective highlighting strategy and discuss the purpose of the activity.

2. Read through the selection first.

3. Re-read and begin to highlight main ideas and supporting details.

4. Highlight only the facts that are important or the key vocabulary, not the entire sentence.

5. After highlighting, look at what you have highlighted and summarize what you read.

6. Take what was highlighted and write a summary paragraph.

EXAMPLE

When the war began, both sides had advantages and disadvantages. How they would use those strengths and weaknesses would determine the war's outcome. The North enjoyed the advantages of a larger population, more industry, and more abundant resources than the South. It had a better banking system, which helped to raise money for the war. The North also possessed more ships and almost all the members of the regular navy remained loyal to the Union. Finally, the North had a larger and more efficient railway network.

KEY
- Main idea
- Details
- Examples

HOT TIPS

- Be sure you are allowed to mark in the textbook or supplemental material before you begin.

- Use a one-page print version of the main ideas and key vocabulary as a study guide for testing.

- Monitor students to ensure they are not highlighting everything in a paragraph. This is not a help, but a hindrance.

- Set purposes for reading.

STUDENTS WHO BENEFIT
- Are inattentive and have a hard time focusing.
- Need assistance with seeing the "big idea" of the content.
- Enjoy activity-based learning.

© 2016, Stetson & Associates, Inc.

SOCRATIC QUESTIONING
Strategy 40

The purpose of using this method is to help students achieve a deeper understanding about the ideas and values in a text. Through examination and questioning, students construct meaning through disciplined analysis, interpretation, listening and participation.

Sample Rubric!
http://tinyurl.com/ojwv9we

Adapted from: Sample Socratic Seminar Lesson. Dr. Ghiora, Wendy. Posting #333, October 17, 2009. http://teaching4achange.blogspot.com/2009/10/sample-socratic-seminar-lesson.html

HOT TIPS

Before the seminar review the discussion norms:
- Don't raise hands.
- Listen carefully.
- Address one another respectfully and use good eye contact.
- Base opinions on the text.
- Allow everyone a chance to speak.

During the seminar:
- Pose the key question.
- Refocus students on the opening question by restating it if they get off track.
- Encourage everyone to participate.

After the seminar:
- Summarize the main points.
- Guide students in a reflective process.

IMPLEMENTATION

1. The teacher selects TEXT.
The text selected should contain important, powerful ideas and values at the appropriate level for students. Good discussions occur when students study the text closely in advance, listen actively, share their ideas and questions in response to the ideas and questions of others, and search for evidence in the text to support their ideas. The discussion is not about right answers; it is not a debate. Students are encouraged to think out loud and to exchange ideas openly while examining ideas in a rigorous, thoughtful, manner.

2. The teacher creates a CLASSROOM ENVIRONMENT.
   Steps to Creating Socratic Circles
   1. Teacher assigns a selection of text the day before the activity.
   2. Students read and take notes individually.
   3. The next day, students are divided into two circles. The inner circle reads the text aloud and holds a ten minute discussion, while the outer circle silently observes. The outer circle provides feedback to the inner circle.
   4. Students switch circles and repeat the process.

3. The teacher develops SOCRATIC QUESTIONS.
Prepare several questions in advance in addition to questions students may bring to class. Questions should lead participants into the core ideas and values, and in the use of the text in their answers. Questions must be open-ended, reflect genuine curiosity, and not have only one right answer. Choose one question as the key interpretive question of the seminar to focus on and begin discussion. It is highly recommended that teachers engage students in a final reflection of questions discussed at the end of the seminar process.

© 2016, Stetson & Associates, Inc.

STICKY NOTE QUESTIONS
Strategy 41

Sticky Note Questions is a reading strategy in which students interact with text prior to, during and after reading to improve their comprehension. Students engage with the text and focus on specific aspects of the reading process while applying reading strategies. Students are actively participating in reading while strategically adding the sticky notes.

Adapted from: Classroom Strategies for Interactive Learning, Doug Buehl, 2008. Comprehension Shouldn't Be Silent, M. Kelly and N. Clausen-Grace, 2007. Creating Independence Through Student-Owned Strategies, C. Santa, L. Havens, B. Valdes, 2004.

IMPLEMENTATION

BEFORE READING
Students write questions they predict will be answered by the text on a sticky note, and place it where they predict the question may be answered.

DURING READING
As students read, they use sticky notes to mark parts of the reading selection they have questions about, want to discuss, enjoyed, found humorous, want to remember, etc.

AFTER READING
In pairs, small groups or as a whole class, discuss parts that were marked and why.

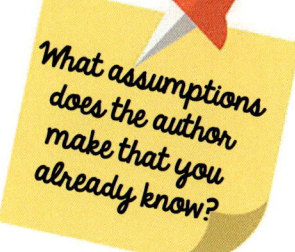

HOT TIPS

- Model process for students using the think-aloud process explaining your rationale for marking parts of the text.

- Use different colored sticky notes for different types of notations (key vocabulary, terms students do not understand, information that supports an opinion, etc).

- Have students work in pairs and pose their questions to one another.

- After the discussion, hold students accountable by having them write a summary of their discussion, comprehension of the material, reactions, etc.

EXAMPLES

- What is the author saying?
- How did the author explain the information?
- What assumptions does the author make that you already know?

TASK ANALYSIS
Strategy 42

Task analysis is the process of teaching a skill by breaking it into smaller steps. Once the small steps are identified, the skill is taught by forward or backward chaining. Task analysis can be used with any academic or functional skill. Task analysis allows the teacher or paraeducator to evaluate the student's performance and understand exactly what skills need to be taught.

HOT TIPS

- Gradually increase the steps completed by the student as he/she masters them.

- Keep documentation of the student's performance.

- Use task analysis if a student is having difficulty learning a new skill.

- Once you have analyzed a task, keep a copy in case another student needs to learn that skill.

IMPLEMENTATION

1. The teacher identifies the skill to be taught.

2. Write down each step in the sequence of completing the task.

3. The teacher presents the task to the student and observes to see which, if any, steps he/she can complete independently. This provides a starting point for teaching.

4. Teach the skill by forward or backward chaining until the student can complete the entire task independently.

EXAMPLE

FORWARD CHAINING (Add steps starting with the first step)

1.	The student completes step 1 and the adult finishes the task.
2.	When the student has mastered step 1 add step 2. Now the student completes steps 1 and 2 and the adult finishes the task.
3.	Continue adding steps until the student is doing all of the steps in the task and the adult is not doing any steps.

BACKWARD CHAINING (Add steps starting with the last step)

1.	The adult does the task except for the last step. The student does the last step.
2.	When this is mastered, add another step for the student. Now the student does the last two steps.
3.	Continue adding steps until the student is doing the entire task and the adult is not doing any.

© 2016, Statson & Associates, Inc.

TEXT QUEST
Strategy 43

A text quest is a scavenger hunt activity to guide students through a pre-reading survey of a text, unit, chapter, article or story to activate prior knowledge, set a purpose for reading and acquaint the student with the text format. This is a "front loading" technique as it points out specific features of a text, helps students notice the text structure, and encourages identification of key points.

IMPLEMENTATION

1. The teacher previews the textbook or chapter, highlighting interesting items, critical components or features of the text and the organization of the book or chapter.
2. The teacher creates the text quest of 8-10 items students are to find in the quest.
3. Students may work independently, in pairs or in small groups to complete the quest.
4. Conduct a whole group discussion regarding the information and the organization of the textbook reading.

EXTENSION: Create and save your text quests on the computer. Share the process with grade-level partners.
www.wix.com
www.audiobooks.com

EXAMPLE

1. How many units are in the book?
2. Study the cover of the book. Write 3-5 sentences that explain why the authors chose to put these pictures on the cover.
3. Go to page 78 and find the answer to the question, "What causes evaporation?"
4. What is the difference between the glossary and the index?
5. What picture is on page 121? What are three facts that are included in the picture?
6. What are the bold-faced words on page 220?
7. What is the last page of Chapter 9? How do you suppose this might help you with your reading?
8. What page and information caught your interest?

HOT TIPS

• Be sure to highlight aspects that are interesting to students when creating a text quest.
• This strategy helps students focus on what is important.
• Students can complete this strategy independently, in pairs or in a group.
• Once students become more proficient at this skill, have them create chapter tours or text quests.

BEFORE: Text quest could be a preview of information to be covered or discussed.
DURING: Could possibly be utilized to find specific answers for a class discussion.
AFTER: Completed text quest could serve as organized notes for summarizing information or studying for a test.

© 2016, Stetson & Associates, Inc.

THINK FAST
Strategy 44

This strategy requires no preparation and allows the teacher to re-engage learners quickly. During a longer lesson, the teacher stops instruction for a short period of time and has the students think fast and either write or draw a word, picture, or short phrase that will help them remember something they just heard. Think Fast can be used to make predictions, connect prior learning or to reflect on what the students just learned.

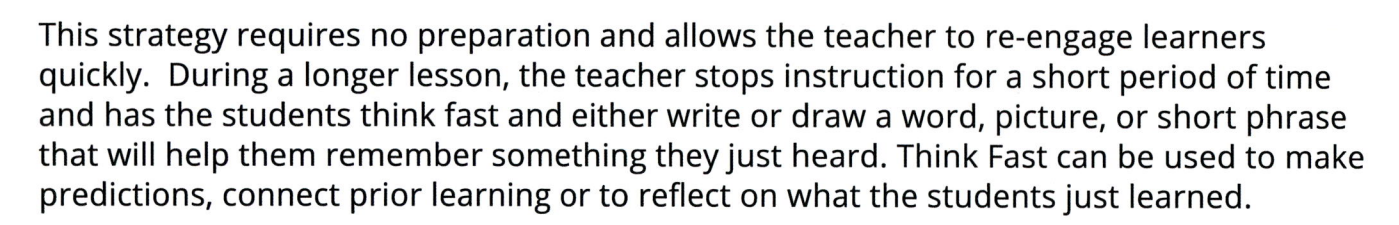

HOT TIPS

- Use this strategy to connect prior learning.

- Break up whole group lessons by interjecting a Think Fast activity.

- Let the class create a Class Mosaic with their drawings.

- Begin with very short time increments and extend the time as students become comfortable with this strategy.

- Let the students use colored pencils to increase visual interest.

IMPLEMENTATION

1. Get the students' attention and tell them to "Think Fast".

2. Once students are listening, give a specific directive such as:
   a. Draw a picture that will help you remember what you learned.
   b. Write one thing you just learned.
   c. Write one sentence that will help you remember _____.

3. Provide students a short period of time to write or draw.

4. The teacher can continue instruction or have the class share what they have written/drawn before continuing.

Adapted from: Total Participation Techniques
Tompkins, Gail E. (1994). Teaching Writing: Balancing Process and Product. 2nd ed. New York: Macmillan College Publishing Company, Inc.

EXAMPLE

1. Before beginning a lesson on figurative language, have students write one example of a metaphor.

2. During a lesson on finding the main idea, have students draw a picture that shows what the story is about.

3. After a lesson on fractions, have students write one word that will help them remember what they just learned.

© 2016, Stetson & Associates, Inc.

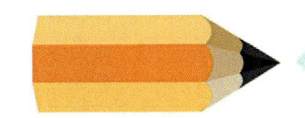

THINK PAIR SHARE
Strategy 45

This strategy encourages students to reflect on a specific concept, partner with another student, and share their ideas and thoughts. Students can be placed into partners in a variety of ways, depending on the arrangement of the room and whether or not the teacher wants the students to get out of their desks or remain seated during the strategy. Think Pair Share can be adapted in many ways in the classroom to build opportunities for students to reflect, share, and be ready for more instruction.

Think-Pair-Share (Lyman, 1981): An Equity Pedagogical Best Practice to Increase and Vary Student Participation in the Classroom.

IMPLEMENTATION

1. Tell the class to THINK about a specific topic. The students should think silently for 1 minute.

2. When time is up, direct the students to PAIR up with another student and SHARE their thoughts. Set a timer for a specific amount of time or cue the students when it is time to get their attention.

3. Debrief quickly by having a few students share with the whole group.

4. Continue with the lesson.

HOT TIPS

• If students are seated in rows they can pair up with their shoulder buddy or elbow partner.

• Have students write down their ideas before pairing and sharing to increase accountability.

• During the debrief, have students share what their partner said. "Sally said ..." instead of sharing only what they wrote down.

• Use music. When the music stops students stop sharing.

• Don't forget to give time to think. Kids need time to process the prompt and come up with their response before they are ready to share.

EXAMPLE

During a lesson on the water cycle the teacher tells the students to think about the steps in the water cycle, pair with their elbow buddy, and share.

During debrief, have partners pair up with another group for a new group of four. The new group shares their ideas.

Build in opportunities for movement by having them pair up with someone on the other side of the room.

© 2016, Stetson & Associates, Inc.

TIERED LEARNING
Strategy 46

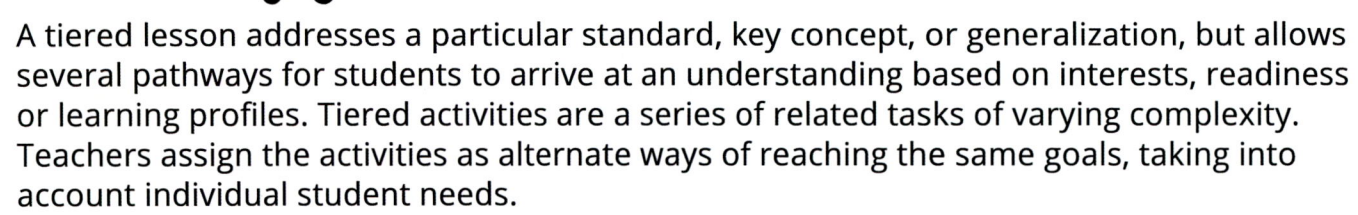

A tiered lesson addresses a particular standard, key concept, or generalization, but allows several pathways for students to arrive at an understanding based on interests, readiness or learning profiles. Tiered activities are a series of related tasks of varying complexity. Teachers assign the activities as alternate ways of reaching the same goals, taking into account individual student needs.

Example adapted from: Differentiated Instruction in the Foreign Language Classroom: Meeting the Diverse Needs of all Learners. Toni Theisen, Loveland, Co. The Communiqué PDF: Page 5

HOT TIPS

- Focus is on maximum growth & continued success.

- Teachers form tiers based on the assessment of students' abilities to master the content.

- Student & teacher are collaborators in learning.

- Teacher understands, appreciates & builds on student differences.

- Encourages the student to explore ideas at a level that builds on prior knowledge & prompts continued growth.

- Builds understanding, engages & challenges students.

IMPLEMENTATION

1. Identify the grade level and subject for the lesson.
2. Identify the curricular standard being targeted.
3. Identify key concepts and generalizations.
4. Assess to determine that students have the necessary background knowledge to be successful in the lesson.
5. Determine the area to tier.
6. Determine the type of tiering you will do: readiness, interest, or learning profile.
7. Based on your choices above, determine how many tiers you will need and develop the lesson.
8. Develop the assessment component to the lesson.

EXAMPLE

TOPIC: Clothing
LANGUAGE & LEVEL: French III
Students use clothing vocabulary in real world contexts. They are able to describe in detail, suggest clothing items, persuade, compare and contrast and encourage. Students apply different social registers for friends and work situations. Students know about the impact of the French fashion industry and are aware of the styles of clothing in other Francophone countries. Students know how to use currency. Students are able to research information about the clothing industry using the Internet.

TARGETED STANDARDS
COMMUNICATION: Presentational Mode
CULTURES: Products and Perspectives
CONNECTIONS: Access to information, Other subject areas
COMPARISONS: Concept of culture
COMMUNITIES: Within and beyond the school
BACKGROUND: Students have studied clothing, vocabulary & descriptive adjectives. They can use direct and indirect object pronouns when identifying clothing. They can persuade, encourage and suggest using commands, conditional and subjunctive. Students are aware of the Francophone countries and are aware of the different styles of clothing and the roles of clothing in the culture and can relate this information to a diversity perspective. They have done a variety of activities and assessments. They have also done web quest research activities on the Internet. Therefore, these activities are designed for the readiness level of the students.

TIER 1 ASSIGNMENT (Complex & Abstract)	TIER 2 ASSIGNMENT (Somewhat Complex & Concrete)	TIER 3 ASSIGNMENT (Very Concrete)
Your group works for a business training institute. Your task is to write two role-play scenarios for students to use as a practice when dealing with a variety of customers in a clothing store. You are to set-up each scenario and for each one, write a practice conversation between a "challenging" client and a vendor. These conversations would be used by business school students to practice appropriate interactions between a challenging client and a vendor. The conversations should encourage and persuade. Submit a written copy and be ready to present one conversation, without notes, as a model for the class.	Your group comprises the "Rules Committee" for a high school in Montreal, Canada. You have been assigned to write a small section of the school handbook that explains the school's dress code. For this handout, write a brief general statement about the dress policy. Then write 12 school rules discussing the dos and don'ts of school dress. Describe the clothes that are acceptable or those that are not. Turn in a typed copy of the descriptions and the dress code for publication in the school handbook. Also, create a poster with the 12 guidelines, and be ready to present to the class.	You work for an ad agency whose job is to create a mini catalog and a sales ad for one of the big department stores in Paris. Using magazine pictures, drawings and/or pictures from the Internet, create a mini-catalog with 12 clothing items. You decide on the theme, age, or gender group. Describe each item using models from previous readings. Price the item in Euros. Type the descriptions and neatly arrange the catalog to make it appealing to customers. Also create an ad promoting at least two of the items on sale. Be creative in your design, and be ready to present both the catalog and the ad to the class.

© 2016, Stetson & Associates, Inc.

VISUAL SCHEDULES
Strategy 47

A visual schedule is a set of pictures or words that communicates a sequence of activities a student is to complete independently. Visual schedules teach independence and choice making by allowing students to work without having an adult provide continual prompting.

IMPLEMENTATION

1. Determine what level of symbol the student understands such as, photographs, drawings or words.
2. Select a format for the schedule. It can be written out or display a sequence of vertical or horizontal symbols.
3. Select the tasks that will appear on the schedule.
4. If using pictures, create two sets that represent each task. One copy of each picture goes on the student's schedule and the other copy is placed on the activity so the student can match the pictures.
5. Place a small piece of Velcro on the back of the pictures that will be placed on the student's schedule. The other side of the Velcro is placed on a piece of poster board, cardstock, or other material. The student is expected to move the pictures.
6. Place an envelope or other small container at the end of the schedule board. The student will return the pictures here when the task is complete.

USING THE SCHEDULE

1. Sequence tasks on the schedule in logical order.
2. Ensure necessary materials are easily accessible to student.
3. Prompt the students to check their schedules.
4. The student moves to the schedule, looks at the first picture, gathers materials, completes the activity, returns the picture and goes to the next picture.
5. If a student stops working or needs prompting, remind him to check his schedule and continue until all tasks are completed.

HOT TIPS

- Allow students to select the order they complete the activities.
- If a student can read, use words on the schedule.
- If a student can't match pictures, you will need to teach this skill before starting.
- Visual schedules can also be used to structure the school day so the student always knows what is coming next.

Brush your teeth.

Wash your hands.

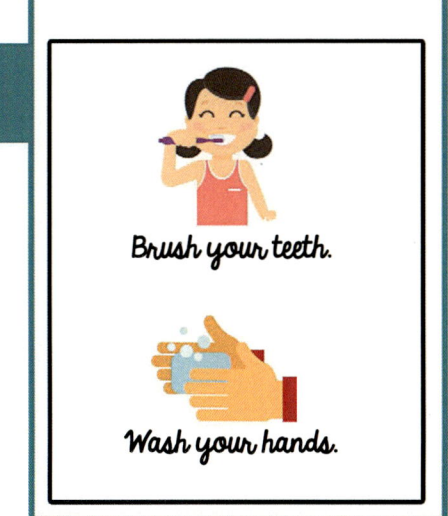

© 2016, Stetson & Associates, Inc.

WINDOWPANE
Strategy 48

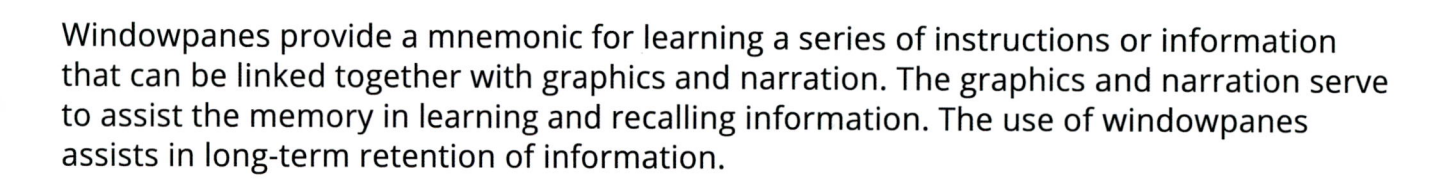

Windowpanes provide a mnemonic for learning a series of instructions or information that can be linked together with graphics and narration. The graphics and narration serve to assist the memory in learning and recalling information. The use of windowpanes assists in long-term retention of information.

HOT TIPS

• Assists visual & kinesthetic learners to better acquire and retain information.

• Teaches abstract concepts with more ease by offering a concrete representation.

• Promotes cooperative interaction among students.

• When used with a timed component, aids with fluency and retention.

• Can be used for review, new content or as a skill-builder for fluency.

IMPLEMENTATION

1. The teacher prepares a completed windowpane with six to nine panes for modeling.
2. Students fold paper into six or nine squares.
3. The teacher reveals the windowpanes one at a time for the students to draw on their own papers. As each pane is revealed, describe what the graphic represents and its significance or relevance. Link each drawing in some way.
4. After revealing, explaining and allowing the students to draw each of the panes, have them review with a partner to check for accuracy. Set a time limit of 1-2 minutes.
5. Do a quick review using the teacher model. Ask the students to put away their papers, so they will be unable to look at their graphics. Practice the windowpane orally.
6. For added practice, a game can be made out of the windowpane. The teacher can give teams an envelope with a cut up windowpane, plus one extra piece. When the teacher says, "Go", teams are to put the panes in order while timing themselves to see how long it takes. When all the teams are finished, reveal the master windowpane to check for accuracy.
7. Students will practice several times, but each time the goal will be to beat the previous time. Teams can take 1 minute to discuss their strategy for decreasing their time. The teacher gives the signal to begin.

EXAMPLE

© 2016, Stetson & Associates, Inc.

WORD ALERT
Strategy 49

The purpose of this strategy is to activate students' prior knowledge of a concept or vocabulary used in text. Students assess their knowledge of words or concepts using a template.

Adapted from: Comprehension Shouldn't be Silent, Michelle Kelley & Nicki Clausen-Grace, 2007

IMPLEMENTATION

1. The teacher selects words or concepts important for comprehending a selection of text.
2. The teacher adds these words to the Word Alert template (see below), leaving space for students to add words.
3. Prior to reading, the students complete the first three columns of the template. If the student indicates that he knows the word, he writes what he thinks it means and how he knows it. If the student does not know the word, he highlights the word so he can focus on it while reading.
4. While reading, the student looks for confirmation of the definition, noting the page number where he found it for future reference.
5. After completing the reading, the student discusses the words and the relationship to the text's context.

HOT TIPS

• Prior to reading, have students discuss the words and definitions.

• After reading, have students discuss the definitions and text evidence.

• Ask students to write a summary of the words, definitions and why they are critical to the concept.

• This strategy targets the following reading comprehension skills: predicting, questioning, summarizing and making connections.

EXAMPLE

Word Alert Template

Name: _____ Date: _____
Text or Book Title: _____

Critical Word	Do you know the word? Y/N	What is your definition?	If Unknown Check & Highlight	Definition confirmation or text evidence (pg. #)

© 2016, Stetson & Associates, Inc.

WORDSPLASH
Strategy 50

This strategy can be utilized to activate prior knowledge before teaching a lesson, to conduct a pre-assessment, as a note-taking guide, as a post-assessment, as a prediction activity or as a vocabulary lesson. Students can complete the WordSplash independently, in pairs or in a small or large group.

HOT TIPS

- The words can be paired with pictures or visuals for students working on literacy skills.

- The first time using this strategy, have students make a prediction based on their knowledge of words. Students can make adjustments to their predictions.

- This activity can be completed independently, in a group or in pairs. If done in a group, one student can record the predictions.

- Use a cloud based program such as Google Docs, ABCYA.com Word Cloud for Kids or a word processing software on your computer to make the WordSplash even more interesting.

IMPLEMENTATION

1. Identify the key vocabulary words or concepts related to the topic.

2. Create a WordSplash by "splashing" the words on the page at different angles using different fonts and colors.

3. Have students predict each word's relationship to the topic. Be sure to tell them that at this point in time you just want a prediction; make the parallel between scientists making a hypothesis. Initially, some students are reluctant to make predictions as they are so conditioned to always provide the right answer.

4. Have students read the selection or you may provide explicit instruction on the topic.

5. Ask students to return to their WordSplash and modify predictions as needed. Once students are familiar with this strategy, they can create their own WordSplash.

EXAMPLE

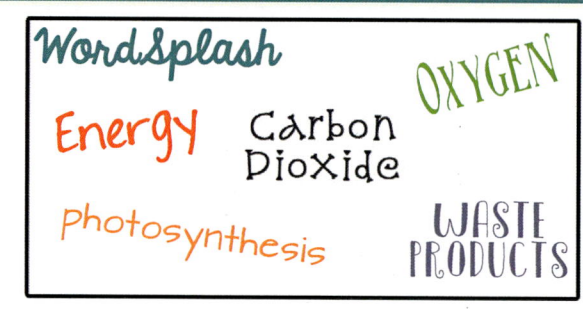

WordSplash

Energy   Carbon Dioxide   OXYGEN

photosynthesis   WASTE PRODUCTS

© 2016, Stetson & Associates, Inc.